A LAYMAN'S GUIDE TO
NEW AGE
&
SPIRITUAL
TERMS

Elaine Murray

Blue Dolphin Publishing
1993

Published by Blue Dolphin Publishing, Inc.
P.O. Box 1908, Nevada City, CA 95959

ISBN: 0-931892-53-8

Library of Congress Cataloging-in-Publication Data

Murray, Elaine, 1941–
    A layman's guide to New Age and spiritual terms / Elaine
Murray.
        p.   cm.
    Includes bibliographical references.
    ISBN 0-931892-53-8 : $12.95
    1. New Age movement—Encyclopedias. I. Title.
    BP605.N48M87 1992   92-41892
    133'.03—dc20   CIP

Cover design: Jeff Case

Printed in the United States of America by
Blue Dolphin Press, Inc., Grass Valley, California

PRINTING 10   9   8   7   6   5   4   3   2   1

For Wesley,
my soulmate
and master
of
the two-by-four

* * * * * * * * * *

For Andrew and Heather
my two beautiful Star Children.

Table of Contents

Introduction

I have been a student of metaphysics for the past twenty years. My search for answers has led me to read a multitude of books, attend seminars and lectures, sit for spiritual development classes, attend a spiritualist church, and take special courses relating to the field of parapsychology. Nowhere did I find a dictionary to help me through the vocabulary I encountered. Terms and ideas were scattered throughout a hundred different books. I have attempted to put some of the things I have learned all under one roof, in alphabetical order, and I have included some personal comments and experiences, lest things get too technical.

Much more could be said about each term. I purposely excluded most psychological terms and negative words, and cited only a few pioneers. You are welcome to write to me c/o the publisher if you have any suggestions.

I hope the words I have chosen (or which have chosen me) will help beginners who are just now taking their first steps down the path of enlightenment. There might be a new thing or two, even for the seasoned traveller. Whatever the case . . . enjoy the journey . . . and may you find LOVE, the ultimate destination.

—E.M.

A

Absent Healing
Adept
Affirmation
Age of Aquarius
Akashic Records
Alpha State
Amen
Amulet
Angels and Archangels
Ankh
Apocrypha
Apparition
Apports
A.R.E.
Aromatherapy
Ashram
Aspirant
Astral Body
Astral Plane
Astral Projection
Astrology
Astronomy
Atlantis
At-one-ment
Attunement

Aura
Automatic Writing
Avatar
Awareness

ABSENT HEALING

Absent healing is a healing which results from the sending of healing thoughts, prayers, or energy to and for someone who is absent from the person or group sending the healing.

Comment: I guess my first encounter with the idea of absent healing happened during my childhood. When I was nine years old, I witnessed the death of my younger brother, Lloyd. A steel-wheeled farm wagon, loaded with bags of grain, ran over his head, crushing it. Dad pumped cold water from the well and washed the terrible wounds but he could not save my brother. Lloyd died in minutes. Father's grief was inconsolable.

My father had a difficult time adjusting to my brother's death, and began his spiritual search which would bring him some peace of mind. Consequently, for the next few years, I was taken to church twice every Sunday. We must have visited every Protestant church within a radius of fifty miles. I used to hear people praying at these meetings that so-and-so might be healed of their afflictions. It was at that young age that I began to believe absent healings were possible.

In the '70s I took a Mind Awareness course from a Toronto-based organization. We were taught how to visualize candidates for absent healing. I surprised myself with the accuracy of these visualizations.

It was not until some years later that I had a real confirmation that absent healings can be so dramatic. At that time, I sat with a meditation circle. The group decided to work on healings for several months. One night the name "Kirby" was given to the group. He was a young boy. I immediately had trouble breathing—to the point where it frightened me. When I finally realized the sensation was foreign to my usual responses . . . the shortness of breath vanished.

"Good grief," I exclaimed. "Does this boy have asthma?"

It turned out Kirby was asthmatic, and after the group sent healing, he was free from attacks for some time thereafter.

ADEPT

An *adept* is someone who has particular skills or proficiency in a certain subject or activity. An adept is considered a master in applying his knowledge of cosmic laws and principles to the affairs of his life. He is said to have attained illumination.

AFFIRMATION

An *affirmation* is a positive declaration about something you wish to change or create in your life.

Example: I am a beautiful woman/handsome man because I have only beautiful thoughts and feelings. Happiness makes me beautiful now.

Example: I am alert to my anger responses. I respond to all situations with reason. I am no longer a child who reacts childishly. I am a mature person. I react with love, wisdom, and understanding.

Comment: Affirmations can say anything you want them to say. Make up your own. Write them down on a piece of paper, and repeat them daily. Watch the results.

AGE OF AQUARIUS

The concept of an *Age* exists within ancient spiritual traditions. It is always 2000 years in duration, and denotes a change process that is occurring during that period for the evolution of consciousness, for the good of all. The energy that entered this plane 2000 years ago, at the beginning of what astrology calls the *Piscean Age,* was *Agape* (brotherly and sisterly love)—love of one human being for another simply because each is worthy of love and part of the same human family. That energy is only now being consciously accepted in any general manner. It has taken us the entire *Age* for us to "get it."

Christ brought this love-energy to our world about 2000 years ago, and we humans have been working on it ever since. We are just beginning to open to sisters and brothers everywhere. By the year A.D. 2000, maybe we will have developed that critical mass of love energy that is needed for the next Age: *the Age of Aquarius*. This time the message expands to, "not only are we brothers and sisters . . . we are one." The *Piscean Age* taught us we are all connected; we must love one another as ourselves. The "other" is an illusion. You and I are one consciousness reflected in an infinite rainbow of seeming difference; all is one.

The *Age of Aquarius* is referred to as the "New Age," but you can see there is nothing new about it. It is simply an evolution in man's thinking. *New Age* thinking asks that each person take respon-sibility for everything that happens in life, because everything in life is connected. We must learn to love ourselves, for out of love for one's self, comes love for others. The person who is bound by a negative image, wound up in self-doubt, does not permit time or energy to really care about anyone else.

When we confront ourselves, and understand the causes for our feelings of hatred and anger, we can change the feelings, or even let them go. That involves taking responsibility for what we feel; be-coming more consciously aware of why we feel what we do. In doing so, we are expanding our conscious awareness. To use a *New Age* term—we are "raising our consciousness" about our unconscious perceptions of who we are, and how we are behaving. Peace for the world begins with peace within ourselves. The biggest hurdle is learning how to create that inner peace and balance. There is no doubt: we are leaving the *Piscean Age* symbolized by the sign of the fish, and entering the Aquarian Age symbolized by the water bearer.

AKASHIC RECORDS

The word *akashic* is derived from a Sanskrit word which means "Primary Substance," that out of which all things are formed. This primal substance is everywhere present. It is the *Universal Mind* of which metaphysicians speak. The *akashic records*, then, refer to the indelible record of all events, occurrences, and knowledge which is part of the Cosmic Consciousness. All things which have come to pass, or which will happen, are established in the Akashic records. Every thought, feeling, and action in this world of experience is recorded. Some think of the Akashic records as a book for each person in a grandiose library of sorts.

Access to the Akashic records is difficult. One must attune the conscious mind with the Cosmic Consciousness.

Comment: It would sure be a lot easier if the Divine Intelligence used a computer to store the Akashic records—and all we had to do is push a button for our own personal print-out.

ALPHA STATE

An *alpha state* is when the brain waves fluctuate between seven and twelve cycles per second. Slowing our brain waves to this level is desirable for many reasons: meditation, creativity, health projects, and biofeedback . . . to name a few. (*See* BIOFEEDBACK and BRAIN WAVE FREQUENCIES.)

AMEN

Amen is a Hebrew word introduced into Egyptian mystic rites which was used to express the hidden and invisible God. *Amon* was used to designate the god of Thebes which is associated with life and reproduction. *Amen-Ra* came to express the name and hierarchy of a powerful god among the Egyptians. *Amen-Ra* was the Egyptian sun god.

Amenhotes IV changed his name to Khuen-Aten because of the significance of the term "Amen."

When used in modern religious practices, the term means: verily, truly, certainly, may it be so, or so it is! It is used after a prayer to express approval.

The origin of the word "amen" is found in the Sanskrit AUM and also OM.

Comment: I think we should update the word AMEN. If it were changed to RIGHT-ON! . . . it would sure grab the attention of our younger generation.

AMULET

An *amulet* is a stone designed to be worn for protection. It can be inscribed with a design or be part of the design. Examples include: cross, heart, star, ankh, and pictures of a master, angel, or spiritual teacher.

ANGELS and ARCHANGELS (*Also see* FAIRIES)

The word *angel* comes from the Greek work *angelos*, meaning *messenger*. Thus, *angels* are heavenly beings who mediate between God and humankind.

Belief in angels is ancient and widespread. In Jacob's dream of the ladder, angels climbed and descended. When Jacob wrestled with the Angel, he engaged in a primordial battle with his inner self.

Angels are not peculiar to Christian traditions alone. The prophet Mohammed received the *Koran* from God via the archangel Gabriel. (Gabriel also told Mary she would be Christ's mother.) An archangel is an angel of high rank. Mohammed claimed that Gabriel was beautiful, with a whiteness brighter than snow. His hair fell in long tresses, and a crown of light encircled his brow.

The Peruvian hawk-spirit *Koakiti* appears to the shaman as a winged man. The four Thunderbirds of the North American Sioux are seen as winged men.

Angels belong to another order of being, but the boundary is permeable. Angels like Lucifer, who refused to bow to God's new creation, may fall or be cast down; likewise, humans may ascend.

"Guardian Angels" are related to our inner guide, our intuition, and help steer us through a course in life.

The *Seraphim* (one of nine in the order of angels) inspires mortals towards divine love.

Comment: Mankind has always been fascinated with these beings of light. I am no exception. Tulma is a being of light who visits me. (*See* DEVELOPMENT *and* GUIDES). I wonder if Tulma could be classified as an angel?

I will leave this subject of angels with one parting thought . . . a verse from the Bible. In Hebrews 13: 2, it states: "Be not forgetful to entertain strangers, for thereby some have entertained angels unawares."

ANKH

The *Ankh* is the Egyptian symbol of life. It is composed of a "T" crowned with a loop or "0," which denotes the union of man with woman. (*See* CROSS)

APOCRYPHA

The *Apocrypha* is a collection of books used to form part of the Bible, but are seldom printed as part of the Bible any longer. This is partly due to the fact that the Puritans disapproved of them. They began to demand copies of the King James Version omitting them as early as 1629.

Although the *Apocrypha* did not form part of the Hebrew Bible, they were part of the Bible of the early church. The early church used the Greek version of the Jewish Bible, called the Septuagint, and these books (the *Apocrypha*) were all in that version. From there, they passed into Latin and the great Latin Bible edited by St. Jerome about A.D. 400. This Bible was called the Vulgate, which became the Authorized Bible of western Europe and England . . . and remained so for a thousand years. Jerome found that these books were not in the Hebrew Bible, so he called them the *Apocrypha*, the hidden or secret books.

These books were scattered throughout the Vulgate, just as they were through the Greek Bible. They were also scattered through versions made from the Vulgate.

Luther separated them in his German Bible of 1534 from the rest of the Old Testament, and put them after it.

Coverdale followed the same course the following year, in the first printed English Bible of 1535. The English Authorized Bibles, the Great Bible, the Bishops', and the King James, all followed suit. The Catholic English Old Testament of 1610, however, followed the Vulgate arrangement and left them scattered among books which are included in the Protestant Old Testament. It still contains them; but on the Protestant side both American and British Bible Societies took a definite stand against their publication (1827) and they have since, almost disappeared.

The Apocrypha forms a necessary link between the Old Testament and the New Testament. It is indispensable to a student of the New Testament because it forms the prelude, and the background. The Apocrypha includes:

1. The First Book of Esdras
2. The Second Book of Esdras
3. The Book of Tobit
4. The Book of Judith

5. The Additions to the Book of Esther
6. The Wisdom of Solomon
7. Ecclesiasticus or the Wisdom of Sirach
8. The Book of Baruch
9. The Story of Susanna
10. The Song of the Three Children
11. The Story of Bel and the Dragon
12. The Prayer of Manasseh
13. The First Book of Maccabees
14. The Second Book of Maccabees.

APPARITION

An *apparition* is a strange figure which appears suddenly. Some people refer to them as ghosts. Sometimes they appear to be made up of a filmy white substance. When something becomes visible, which we generally consider to be invisible, we call it an *apparition*.

Comment: I have a friend who sees apparitions along the highway where there has been an accident. She says they appear solid, just like real people, except at night, the headlights shine right through them. She used to be frightened that she might run into them, until she learned to discern between the physical and an apparition.

APPORTS

Apports are any objects which materialize out of thin air, into something solid like a stone. This usually occurs during a development class or while sitting in a séance.

When apports have served their purpose, they often dematerialize, returning from matter back into pure energy.

Comment: Sounds like something right out of *Star Trek* doesn't it? I thought so too, until one night in Brantford, Ontario. I had been sitting for some months in a development circle, held at Hope Memorial Spiritualist Church. One evening, we all agreed to use the energy, for some form of physical manifestation of spirit. After "raising the vibrations," as the term goes, I could suddenly hear something fall to the floor from the area of the ceiling. At the same time, one of the collapsible trumpets folded and hit the floor with a thump. Later, two pink stones were discovered at the feet of two individuals who sat in the circle. I was impressed. Some people claim they have received rings as apports. Generally, the apports tend to be small in nature.

A.R.E.

A.R.E. stands for the Association for Research and Enlightenment which has its headquarters in Virginia Beach, Virginia. The headquarters houses the many files containing the transcripts of the Edgar Cayce readings. There are 14,879 readings recorded and indexed in the library of the A.R.E. These transcripts are about everything from health to the direction an individual might travel in the future. These transcripts are available for the public to read.

AROMATHERAPY

Aromatherapy is the art and science of healing with essential oils made from the aromatic parts of flowers, herbs, fruits, spices, resins and woods.

Through inhalation and the sense of smell, the aromas reach deep into the brain's limbic system (the emotional center of the brain) and trigger physical and emotional healings, mood shifts and associations that deeply affect feelings and health. Working on aspects of the physical, mental and spiritual bodies, the botanical oils induce aesthetic pleasure and reduce psychological stress. They also heal physical ailments with their anti-viral, anti-bacterial, hormonal, vitamin and antiseptic properties.

Today's aromatherapy applications are derived from ancient cultures such as the Greek, Roman and Egyptian. Aromatic oils are used in environmental fragrancing through diffusers, hydrosols, scented candles and potpourris. They are also widely used in bath and massage oils and a wide variety of cosmetics and perfumes. Since essential oils are so concentrated, they are usually diluted in vegetable oil for skin application and, when used internally, tiny amounts of pure, food-grade essential oil are diluted in liquid.

Pure rose oil has been successfully used as an anti-depressant and for opening the heart to love. Rosemary is effective in a bath for jet lag. Lavender is a very versatile healer which is used for headaches, nervousness, exhaustion, insomnia and as an antiseptic. It raises the spirits and has been used in a compress for hang-overs. Geranium can help balance emotions. Ylang-ylang is a strong sedative and increases sexual potency. Sassafras kills lice and Clary Sage is used for PMS, menstrual cramps and postpartum depression.

Today in America there is growing interest in Aromatherapy. However, for over sixty years it has been well-established in Europe and is often incorporated by doctors into their medical practices. In France and England a great deal of clinical and medical research is being done. This growing body of scientific knowledge is helping to validate what the ancients learned about healing through intuition and experience.

ASHRAM

An *ashram* is a secluded place for a community of Hindus leading a life of simplicity and religious meditation.

Any secluded place where one can go to restore one's health and spiritual values is often referred to as an ashram.

ASPIRANT

An *aspirant* is anyone yearning or seeking after something lofty or grand. In the case of the metaphysical student, it is someone who is seeking to become "enlightened."

ASTRAL BODY

Our *astral body* is our ethereal double. It co-exists with our physical body, but can leave and travel to the astral or spiritual planes while we are still living on the earth plane. This is possible because a silver cord remains attached from the astral body to the physical body. At death, the cord is broken, and the double remains on the astral plane.

Our astral body often visits the astral plane during sleep. Sometimes we remember bits and pieces of these visits. Some people are capable of leaving their physical body and travelling in their astral body, at will. One such person is Robert Monroe. He found that his astral body could travel through brick walls, and that he could reach any destination merely by thinking about where he wanted to go.

Comment: I remember waking up in the middle of the night. Someone had been talking to me. I didn't remember anything else, except the words this "being" said. They were so profound, I wrote them down without benefit of a light, and immediately fell back asleep. In the morning, I found I had written these words: *"Go, and be the essence of what is."*

ASTRAL PLANE

The *astral plane* is considered to be the lowest of many planes of existence in the world of spirit. It is the closest to the physical plane, as we know it. Above it are higher realms of spirit. The highest plane is unity with God.

After death, the spirit ascends to the astral plane where it rests in a deep sleep, to re-energize after its labors. It sleeps according to its development. A highly evolved soul will require less rest than one in a lower stage of progression. If during its earth life, the spirit has acquired base tendencies, it is likely to go to one of the lower sub-planes upon awakening. An evolved soul will travel to one of the higher planes. Time does not exist on the astral plane as we know it. Past, present, and future are one.

While most people travel to the astral plane only during sleep states, some individuals learn to do this at will and can remember their travels. Some people claim they can raise their mental vibrations to the astral level and literally be in two places at once. One travels from plane to plane by increasing or decreasing one's level of consciousness.

All things on the astral plane are created by the thoughts of its inhabitants and remain, after they have left. The thought forms gradually crumble away as the mental power which created them slowly fades.

During its stay on the astral plane, a spirit receives instruction from higher beings. These higher beings often no longer need to experience another earthly incarnation. When the spirit completes its earthly lessons, it will progress to the advanced planes. It is here where we receive inspiration, guidance, direction and illumination. Sometimes we meet our loved ones who have cast off their earthly bodies. They, too, can give us advice.

Since time and space no longer applies, we can journey back to childhood, visit far-away places, or engage in activities which in earthly time would take longer than one night's rest.

Comment: One night, while sleeping, my father-in-law visited me with a message for his grandson. I gave this message to my son, Andrew. Whether he will act upon it is another matter. Grandpa Murray was a thirty-third degree Mason. His message to Andrew was to join the lodge because: "no one is so secure in the echelons of power, that he cannot stand a little boost." I know this message did not come from my head; I had to look up how to spell "echelon" in the dictionary.

ASTRAL PROJECTION

Astral projection is the conscious projection of the ethereal double (astral body) into the astral plane.

Robert Monroe in his book, *Journeys Out of the Body*, describes several techniques whereby he left his physical body and travelled on the astral planes. Monroe tells us the greatest obstacle he had to overcome was "fear." Fear can turn to panic, then terror. We must consciously pass the fear barrier, because fear inhibits us. Monroe tells us the greatest fear is the "death fear." Because we are separated from the physical body, we think: I am dying! Monroe claims these reactions appear despite any intellectual or emotional training. Only after repeating the projection process eighteen to twenty times did he finally gather enough courage to stay out of his body more than a few seconds, and observe objectively.

There are a number of books which claim they can teach you how to do astral projection. The boundaries can disappear for you if you have the courage and patience. The only way to truly know this extended reality, is to experience it yourself. Good luck! And keep a journal.

Comment: I wish I could astral project at will. I wish I could do that!

ASTROLOGY

Astrology is considered to be a pseudo-science that explains and predicts the course of earthly affairs from observation of the sun, moon, and planets. According to astrology, the temperament and destiny of each person depends on the sign of the zodiac under which he/she is born, and on the continuing aspects of the heavenly bodies.

Astrology was studied among the ancient Egyptians, Hindus, Chinese, Etruscans, and the Chaldeans of Babylon. Observing the influence of the heavenly bodies, and especially that of the sun in ruling the seasons and determining the crops, men came to suppose that the power that ordered the apparent chance of human life resided in the heavens, and that its influence might be read there. For this purpose, the celestial sphere is divided into twelve sectors, the so-called houses of heaven. The influence of each house depends upon the position of the bodies within it, the one containing the stars about to rise being most powerful. The houses differ in their subject matter, each influencing one aspect of the subject's life, such as his longevity, prosperity, marriage, friends, or enemies. Also, certain houses belong to certain planets, the moon or the sun, which, when occupying their houses, have particular powers. Each planet has its own character and influence, good or bad, which determines the personality of the subject. (*See* HOROSCOPE; ZODIAC.)

Characteristics of the sun and planets:

Sun   The sun is the driving force of the universe and giver of life. Its influence is energy and leadership.

Moon   The moon is the female sun and ruler of psychic senses. It is changeable and magnetic. The moon is thought of as the mother goddess, probably from the fact that it takes twenty-eight days to complete its three stages, and this is the length of the menstrual cycle.

Mercury   Mercury is the messenger, bringing reasoning power and perception, restlessness and mental agility.

Venus   Venus is the planet of love and happiness. Artistic talent and passion are associated with Venus.

Mars   Mars is the planet of war and courage, initiative, energy and resourcefulness.

Jupiter   Jupiter is the noble planet. Its influences are faithfulness and generosity.

Saturn Saturn is the slow planet. Its influences are selfishness and deceit.

Uranus Uranus is the impatient planet. Its influences are originality and rashness.

Neptune Neptune is the fluid planet. It influences spiritual and psychic consciousness.

Pluto Pluto is the planet of death and rebirth. It transmits an influence that is forceful and compelling. Pluto expresses Universal Welfare in human thought.

ASTRONOMY

Astronomy is the science of the stars, planets, and all other heavenly bodies. This science deals with their composition, motion, size, and relative position. Astronomy deals with the facts. Here are some basic facts which I have summarized from "A Fantastic Voyage to Neptune" by Sharon Begley and Mary Hager (*Newsweek*, September 4, 1989).

Sun
Diameter: 865,000 miles.
Age: 4.5 billion years.
Satellites: 9 planets

What we know: A rather ordinary, middle-aged star, the gaseous sun may reach 27 million degrees at its core. As of 1989 its eleven-year cycle was approaching a solar maximum, a period marked by frequent sun spots and flares. On earth, some radio waves will be disturbed and the amazing sky streamers called Northern Lights will appear more profusely.

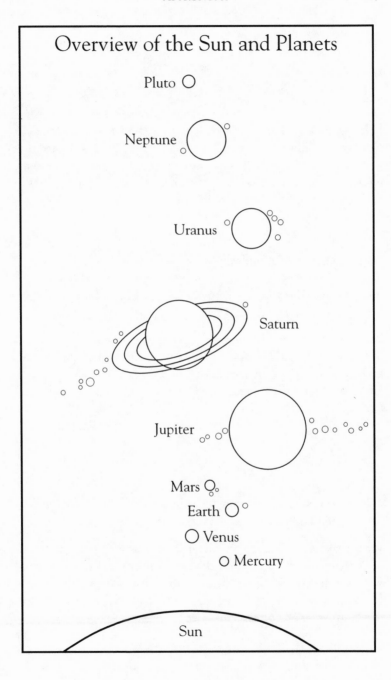

Overview of the Sun and Planets

Pluto

Neptune

Uranus

Saturn

Jupiter

Mars

Earth

Venus

Mercury

Sun

Mercury
Diameter: 3,031 miles
Moons: none
Average distance to sun: 36 million miles
Time to orbit sun: 88 days

What we know: Tiny Mercury, just larger than earth's moon, races
through its elliptical orbit at 110,000 miles per hour—a speed that
keeps it from being drawn into the sun's gravity field. The cratered
planet has no atmosphere; its days are scorching hot and its nights
are frigid.

Venus
Diameter: 7,520 miles
Moons: none
Average distance to sun: 67.2 million miles
Time to orbit sun: 225 days

What we know: Earth's twin in size and mass, searingly hot Venus
is perpetually veiled behind reflective sulfuric-acid clouds. Probes
and radar mapping have pierced the clouds and carbon-dioxide
environment to reveal flat, rocky plains and signs of volcanic activity.

Earth
Diameter: 7,962 miles
Moons: 1
Average distance to sun: 93 million miles
Time to orbit sun: 365 days

What we know: Uniquely moderate temperature and the presence
of oxygen and copious water make earth the only planet in our solar
system to support life as we know it. But, as we despoil the surface
and atmosphere, we run the risk of becoming the galaxy's most
self-destructive creatures.

Mars
Diameter: 4, 222 miles
Moons: 2
Average distance to sun: 141 million miles
Time to orbit sun: 687 days

What we know: The Viking probes failed to find any sign of life. Beneath its thin atmosphere Mars is a barren place, covered with pink soil and boulders. Long ago it was more active: the surface is marked with dormant volcanoes and deep chasms where water once freely flowed.

Jupiter
Diameter: 88,730 miles
Moons: 16
Average distance to sun: 483 million miles
Time to orbit sun: 11.9 years

What we know: Two Pioneer space probes photographed the Great Red Spot on the solar system's largest planet. Voyagers I and II later showed it is an enormous eddy in the turbulent cloud cover. They also spotted dusty rings, three new moons and volcanoes on the moon Io.

Saturn
Diameter: 74,560 miles
Moons: 20 or more
Average distance to sun: 886 million miles
Time to orbit sun: 29.5 years

What we know: Voyager I found that the celebrated rings of the golden giant Saturn are composed of thousands of rippling spiraling bands just 100 feet thick. The moon TITAN has a nitrogen atmosphere and hydrocarbons . . . the necessities of life—but no signs of Titanites.

Uranus
Diameter: 32,560 miles
Moons: 15
Average distance to sun: 1,783 million miles
Time to orbit sun: 84 years

What we know: Watery Uranus is the only planet that lies on its side. One pole, then the other, faces the sun as it orbits. Voyager II found nine dark, compact rings around the planet and a corkscrew-shape magnetic field that stretches millions of miles.

Neptune
Diameter: 29,460 miles
Moons: 8
Average distance to sun: 2.3 billion miles
Time to orbit sun: 165 years

What we know: Voyager II found five rings at Neptune. The outer ring seems studded with icy moonlets, while an inner ring appears narrow and nearly solid. Triton is Neptune's largest moon. It is pink and blue mottled. Triton has a liquid-nitrogen surface and some solid islands of frozen methane, vast ice basins and ridge lines. It has an atmosphere and magnetic field like a planet, but unlike a planet, it does not revolve around the sun. It does, however, orbit backwards.

Neptune is the fourth largest planet. Its blue color results from being filtered through a veil of methane. Neptune, cloaked in a thick haze of hydrogen and helium, is sometimes the farthest planet from the sun, whereas Pluto's path is highly elliptical. Its closest approach to the sun is 2.74 billion miles away, but its farthest approach is 4.57 billion miles in distance. As a result, Neptune is sometimes the furthest from the sun. This will last until 1999, after which it will be Pluto's turn. Neptune will revert to its usual position as the eighth planet from the sun for the next 228 years.

Neptune is streaked by winds that whistle by at up to 400 miles an hour. These push cirrus clouds of frozen methane so fast that one of the wisps has been nicknamed "scooter." A tremendous storm system (christened the Great Dark Spot) marks its southern hemisphere, similar to the Great Red Spot on Jupiter. This system is as big across as Earth. Where Neptune gets its energy for these storms is a mystery, since it receives only one, one-thousandth as much solar radiation as the earth. Neptune has a rocky center about 10,000 miles across, wrapped up in a giant slush ball. The slush is made up of water and liquid methane. Surrounding all this is the atmosphere, composed of hydrogen and helium, with a little methane and ethane. Neptune's energy source could be the most expensive engine in the cosmos. Some astronomers speculate that the methane might, under intense pressures and high temperatures at Neptune's core, decompose into carbon and hydrogen, the carbon then crystallizing into pure diamond. The engine then: a diamond-crusted dynamo powered by dense material falling into the planet's core.

Pluto
Diameter: 1900 miles
Moons: 1
Average distance to sun: 3,666 million miles
Time to orbit sun: 248 years

What we know: The smallest planet, Pluto remains mysterious, but is likely a frozen snowball of water and methane. It follows the most elongated and tilted orbit in the solar system. Pluto's moon, Charon, is nearly half its size, giving the impression of a double planet. After 1999, Pluto will once again be the furthest planet from the sun. (*See* Neptune.)

Comment: About the year 42,000, Voyager II may come within 1.7 light years of the star ROSS 248, a cool, red spot of twinkling gas, one fifth as massive as our sun. In 296,000 years it will pass within 4.3 light years of Sirius, the dog star.

      If one of these stars has planets with life, and they find Voyager II . . . they will find mounted to its side, a copper disc, complete with stylus and cartridge with instructions for playing it. They will hear: greetings from earth in fifty-five languages and one whale dialect;

nature sounds . . . thunder clapping, frogs croaking, and a new-born baby cooing and crying; Jimmy Carter, president of the U.S. at the time saying: "We are attempting to survive our time so that we may live into yours."

ATLANTIS

The story of the lost continent of Atlantis was first told by Plato. Francis Bacon also talked of Atlantis.

Investigations by France and America have proved that there is the contour of a continent on the floor of the Atlantic Ocean.

According to Dr. Frank Alper, Atlantis used to exist across the continental mass now known as the United States, on the east coast. This continent was first populated around 89,000 B.C. These souls in Atlantis basically walked in the Light. There was no faction of a warring nature. At this time, the continent of Mu and Atlantis were connected by tunnels very deep beneath the earth's crust.

The warring faction of Mu (see LEMURIA) made war on Atlantis, resulting in a conflict which eventually destroyed both civilizations, while changes in the earth's vibrations shifted the earth's surface and both continents sank beneath the waters.

Resettlement of Atlantis

In the year 77,777 B.C., ships from alien worlds landed off the coast of what is now Florida. These peoples began to resettle and reconstruct Atlantis beneath the sea. Their journey had taken hundreds of years since they arrived from a distance far beyond this universe. They were mostly families who were born, lived, and reincarnated several times back upon the ships. Their task force had to remain intact. Each ship held several thousand individuals. Upon landing, it took several generations of preparation before the descent into Atlantis was attempted. The source of power for Atlantis was generated through the use of crystals. These crystals were manufactured, but pure as the natural product. Some were twenty-five feet high and ten feet in diameter.

The first 20,000 years of reconstruction was spent in the establishment of energy systems, the establishment of the distribution of power, and in creating food supplies. They built a healing temple with a domed ceiling made of interlocking crystals in varying colors. The healing temple served three functions: a sick person could be energized by the appropriate rays; some accelerated their rate of development by elevating the levels of their vibration frequencies through exposure to higher levels of energy; lastly, a dying individual could be assisted in making the transition rapidly and without hesitation. Certain selected groups had lifespans of several hundred years. This was done by energizing techniques that slow down degeneration of tissue.

The People of Atlantis

The women dressed in gowns both short and long, resembling Grecian dresses and the men wore short tunics. The fabrics were white or tinted in pastels. They wore sandals with thongs wrapped around their legs. The ground was covered with a volcanic ash that would have cut their feet had they not been covered. A rope belt, tied around the waist was their system for denoting rank. One to nine knots were tied on the longer end of the belt. Only those who were the highest among the elders were entitled to have nine knots in their belts. Their diet consisted of fruit, nuts and berries.

When a young man and woman felt a compatibility of vibrations between them, they requested to be united. A Priest or Priestess in the Temple conducted the spiritual union of the couple's vibrations. The couple became "companions," sharing of themselves, but if their vibrational paths altered, they needed only to go to the Temple to have their union dissolved, without cause or concern. It was accepted that individuals grow and evolve at different rates. When the function of their energy exchanges was completed, it was time to establish a new one to insure that growth and evolvement continued.

When a couple bore a child, they kept it until the child turned two years of age. At this time, the child was placed in a nursery under the supervision of women who served in the capacity of "mothers." Here the child grew in Love, in Love for all. It had many mothers and grew to respect them all, in an environment with other children, learning brotherhood and the rules of life. The parents knew they were the instruments to bring the child into existence. They considered the child an individual, not a possession. The children were loved by many and grew in the vibration of love, without jealousy, without frustration, and learned their responsibilities.

One of the ultimate purposes of the society was to allow for total freedom of expression and purpose. They practiced being free souls, without unwarranted restrictions on them.

According to Alper, there are three large caverns containing scientific achievements of the Atlantean period. Two of them are located on the surface of the planet, and one is below the surface in a sealed cavern beneath the waters. Mankind is not ready to receive these gifts at this time, because every gift of Love can be a gift of war. When the time is right, the caverns will be found.

Atlantis was destroyed during its experimental attempts to harness increased power sources which it planned to use in self-defense and in some areas of control. This caused explosions and destruction of certain fire crystals. This ultimately resulted in the chain reaction of energy that destroyed Atlantis. They forgot the source of their most powerful weapon . . . the power of Love. It is said that Atlantis will rise again, but the rising will be one of vibrations.

The islands of Bermuda and Bimini are believed to be remnants of Atlantis.

AT-ONE-MENT

At-one-ment refers to a state of attunement in religious, mystical, and metaphysical practices. The mystic is said to attain at-one-ment when he experiences a union with the Absolute or Cosmos. The term literally means the realization of a state of oneness.

By achieving oneness, unity will come to pass, and with unity . . . peace. Many separations between mankind will fall away. Racial concerns, religious differences, and sexual preferences will no longer be important issues. Each individual will experience his choice. Peace and brotherhood will come to reign on planet earth.

ATTUNEMENT

When you tune any thing, you bring it into harmony or agreement. When you tune a piano, all eighty-eight keys function together. All notes in a given chord will harmonize with each other. When we tune ourselves to God, we are in harmony with ourselves and with our fellow man, and God. We are in a state of at-one-ment and *attunement*.

AURA

The human *aura* is a luminous energy field which surrounds and interpenetrates the physical body. This energy field emanates various colors which are constantly changing according to the mood, health, and emotional state of the individual.

History

Adepts of all religions speak of seeing a light around people's heads. Christian religious paintings portray Jesus and other spiritual figures surrounded by fields of light, sometimes called halos.

This luminous body was first recorded in Western literature by Pythagoreans around 500 B.C. As early as that time, they were aware that its light could produce a variety of effects in the human organism, including the cure of illness. Other properties were observed in the 1800s by Helmont and Mesmer. Count Wilhelm Von Reichenbach experimented during the mid-1800s with the "field," which he called the "odic" force. He found that the force in the human body produced a polarity similar to that present in crystals along their major axes. He described the left side of the body as a negative pole, and the right side as a positive pole. This concept is similar to the ancient Chinese yin and yang principles.

Since 1900, medical doctors have become interested in the aura as well. In the early 1900s, Dr. Walter Kilner discovered that by looking through glass screens stained with dicyanin dye, he could see the aura around the human body. He described three zones: (a) a quarter-inch dark layer closest to the skin, surrounded by (b) a more vaporous layer an inch wide streaming perpendicularly from the body, and (c) further out, a delicate exterior luminosity with indefinite contours about six inches across. Kilner found the appearance of the aura varied from subject to subject depending on age, sex, mental ability, and health. Certain diseases showed as patches or irregularities in the aura. He developed an entire system for diagnosing illnesses from the aura, including: liver infection, tumors, appendicitis, epilepsy, and psychological disturbances like hysteria.

Semyon Kirlian, a Russian electronics expert, discovered a technique in the late 1930s which enabled him to photograph the strange, glowing emanations or force fields. In Kirlian's technique, the object to be photographed was placed on photographic film and sandwiched between two metal plates. A small electric current then passed through the plates and left an illuminated glow on the film. The human aura, when photographed, displayed a mini fireworks show. There were: flares of blue and orange; fiery flashes; streaks of blazing violet. Some lights glittered constantly; others came and went like wandering stars.

Dr. Mikhail Kuzmich Gaikin, a Leningrad surgeon, read about the Kirlians in 1953. Gaikin became interested, so he met with the Kirlians and eventually did some work with them.

The auras which Gaikin observed reminded him of his service as chief surgeon, when he was on the Zabaikal Front in 1945. He had seen Chinese doctors cure what he felt were incurable diseases:

rheumatoid arthritis, epilepsy, and types of deafness. The doctors, he had observed, used the ancient Chinese form of medicine known as acupuncture. Gaikin asked the Chinese how it worked. In Ostrander and Schroeder's book *Psychic Discoveries Behind the Iron Curtain* we read:

> "An energy we call Life Force or Vital Energy circulates through the body on specific pathways," the Chinese told Gaikin. "This Vital Energy can be tapped at seven hundred points on the skin that were mapped out thousands of years ago." The Chinese inserted fine needles at those points to correct imbalances in this supposed primary energy flow, and thus apparently cured disease.
>
> "You see," they said, "these seven hundred points on the skin are in communication with organs deep inside the body and with the whole mental and physiological state of a person. Changing the energy flow on these points changes the Vital Energy deep inside the body."
>
> Dissection showed no trace of the pathways of this so called Vital Energy. It did not make sense to Gaikin, trained in Western medicine. One thing did make sense to him. Patients got better. He studied acupuncture, tried it, and it worked.
>
> . . . in the Kirlians' tiny room, as Gaikin stared at the pictures of a human being under high-frequency fields, it seemed his hunch had paid off. The spots where lights flared most brilliantly appeared to match the acupuncture points the Chinese had mapped out thousands of years ago. Gaikin was excited. Just possibly the Kirlian discovery might give the first scientific confirmation of this five thousand-year-old system of medicine. (p. 227)

The Kirlians were most impressed by the ability to see disease ahead of time; yet this was something the acupuncturists seemed to know all about. There is an old aphorism in Chinese medicine which states: "The superior physician cures before the illness is manifested. The inferior physician can only care for the illness which he was unable to prevent."

Through Gaikin, Kirlian photography and acupuncture got together.

One great problem with acupuncture is locating the tiny treatment points on the skin.(Each point is less than a millimeter wide.)
Dr. Gaikin and Vladislav Mikalevsky (an engineer from Leningrad)
invented an electronic device that pinpoints the acupuncture point
to within a tenth of a millimeter. It is called a "tobiscope." It was
displayed at Expo '67 in Montreal Canada by the Soviet government.

The ability to see the human aura by sensitives has occurred
throughout the centuries, but not until the scientific breakthrough
has this ability been validated. Now perhaps, sensitives and doctors
can work hand in hand to help mankind.

Comment: I believe all children nave a natural ability to see the
human aura. I discovered this quite accidentally. I was teaching
school in a small Ontario village some years ago. At the time, I was
working with children eleven to twelve years of age. Due to a bad
snow storm, the buses were unable to run so only the village children
were present. There were not sufficient numbers to warrant the
teaching of new material. Somehow, the children and I began talking
about colors and auras. The children became interested and wanted
to learn more. How do you see auras? The children wanted to know.
I told them to relax, almost let their eyes go out of focus, and fix their
eyes on someone at the front of the room. I found that about
seventy-five percent could see what I was talking about, although I
could not see auras myself. The children were as excited as I was, and
were only too eager to make chalk drawings of what they saw. Of
course they wanted to know what the colors meant, but I was not
educated enough in the subject to be of much help. I did tell them,
however, that orange tended to be an emotional color while grays
might indicate an impending illness. I found that some children
could not see auras, while some could see them sometimes, and still
others could see auras at all times. One girl could see them very well
and would often thereafter tell me the colors of my aura during recess
break. One day she raised her hand during class and told me that she
thought a certain young boy in the class was not feeling well; she had
been looking at his aura. Billy (his real name) denied feeling any
different than he always did, so the subject was dropped. At break,

the girl came to me privately, and again expressed her concern for Billy. She told me she noticed dark bands in Billy's aura which were not usually there. Oddly enough, Billy was absent from school for the next two days with a case of the flu.

One day I did a relaxation exercise with the children while listening to music. I had asked them to visualize the colors of the spectrum. An eleven-year-old boy came to me afterwards and told me he had difficulty with the short exercise, stating that the only color he could see was red; he wanted to know why. Again, I did not know how to answer him. We were not considering auras, but perhaps there was some connection. I told him I was sorry I could not answer his question, but offered the suggestion that red tends to be a physical color and physically he had been through a lot, and maybe this was the reason he got stuck on red. The child, in fact, had developed cancer of the leg bone and had been through an operation to have his leg amputated in an attempt to arrest the spread of cancer. He had since been fitted with an artificial limb; had progressed quite nicely, and was back at school. The doctors felt confident that all was well. However, a month after this episode, the boy died.

Now, if indeed, an illness can be diagnosed by reading the aura long before there is any physical manifestation, shouldn't we be offering courses in "aura reading" along with math and reading? These young people would nave an invaluable tool long before they ever entered medical school.

Barbara Ann Brennan is one of those gifted adults who can see the human aura with the naked eye. What she has to say in her book *Hands of Light: A Guide to Healing Through the Human Energy Field*, could change your viewpoint forever. She describes seven basic layers to the aura and can see two levels beyond that. She claims the eighth and ninth layers relate to the cosmic level which in turn relates to who we are beyond this lifetime. We are souls reincarnating life after life, slowly progressing in our evolutionary path towards God.

Everything from the seventh level down is, in a sense, a vehicle to guide and support us through this lifetime. In the lower seven layers of our energy field, all the experiences we have had in this lifetime, are stored. These seven layers also contain the blueprints for possible experiences we programmed when planning this particular lifetime. We create our experiences to teach our soul certain lessons we have chosen to learn. Of course, due to our free will, we do not always choose to have all of these experiences.

Here is a brief description of the seven layers and their significance according to Ms. Brennan.

1. First Layer: The Etheric Body

The etheric body is composed of tiny energy lines similar to the lines on a T.V. screen. It has the same structure as the physical body including anatomical parts and organs. Our physical body tissues are shaped by and anchored in this etheric body. This field is prior to, not a result of, the physical body.

This sparkling web of light beams is in constant motion. To clairvoyant vision, sparks of bluish-white light move along its energy lines throughout the entire dense physical body. The etheric body extends from one quarter to two inches beyond the physical body and pulsates about 15-20 cycles per minute.

The color of the etheric body varies from light blue to gray. One can perceive all the organs of the physical body, but they are formed of this scintillating bluish light, similar to a drawing of Spiderman.

2. Second Layer: The Emotional Body

The second auric body is generally associated with feelings. The emotional body roughly follows the outline of the physical body, but its structure is more fluid than the etheric body. It appears to be colored clouds of a fine substance in continual fluid motion. It extends one to three inches from the body. The emotional body contains all the colors of the rainbow. Each chakra (see CHAKRAS) looks like a vortex of a different color and follows the colors of the rainbow:

Chakra one = red
Chakra two = red-orange
Chakra three = yellow
Chakra four = bright grass-green
Chakra five = sky blue
Chakra six = indigo
Chakra seven = white (or violet, sometimes).

3. Third Layer: Mental Body

This body extends beyond the emotional and is composed of still finer substances, all of which are associated with thoughts and mental processes. The mental body usually appears as a bright yellow light radiating about the head and shoulders and extending around the whole body. It extends from three to eight inches from the body. It expands and becomes brighter when its owner is concentrating on mental processes. The mental body is structured. Thought forms appear as blobs of varying bright mass and forms. These thought forms can have additional colors superimposed on them emanating from the emotional body. Habitual thoughts become very powerful "well-formed" forces that can affect our lives.

In Barbara's healing, she claims these three lower auric layers are associated with and metabolize energies related to the physical world. The upper three layers metabolize energies related to the spiritual world. The fourth layer (astral level) is associated with the heart chakra. All spiritual energy must pass through the heart chakra to be transformed into the lower physical energies.

4. Fourth Layer: Astral Level

The astral body is composed of clouds of color more beautiful than those of the emotional body. While the astral tends to have the same set of colors, they are usually infused with the rose light of love. It extends out about one half to one foot from the body.

When people fall in love, beautiful arcs of rose light can be seen between their hearts, and a beautiful rose color is added to the normal golden pulsations of the pituitary gland. Cords grow out of the chakras to connect the couple. When a relationship ends, those cords are torn, sometimes causing a great deal of pain. These cords have to reroot themselves within the self.

A great deal of interaction takes place between people on the astral level. Great blobs of color shoot across the room between people. Some is pleasant, and some is not. You can feel the difference. On the surface, two people may be ignoring each other, but on an energy level, a whole lot of communication is taking place. For example, when a man or woman fantasize about making love with someone, say at a party, there is an actual testing in the energy fields to see if the fields are synchronous and the people are compatible.

5. Fifth Layer: The Etheric Template Body

The fifth layer contains all the forms that exist on the physical plane in blueprint or template form, looking like the negative of a photograph.

It extends out from the body one and one half to two feet. It is the level where sound creates matter. It is at this level that "sounding" in healing is the most effective. To clairvoyant sight, template forms appear as clear or transparent lines on a cobalt blue background, much like an architect's blueprint, only in another dimension. It is as if a form is made by completely filling in the background space, and the empty space left creates the form.

6. Sixth Layer: The Celestial Body

The sixth level extends about two, to two and three-quarter feet from the body. It is the emotional level of the spiritual plane. Through this level we experience spiritual ecstasy. The celestial body appears as a shimmering light of pastel colors. The light has a gold-silver shine and opalescent quality.

7. Seventh Layer: The Ketheric Template or Causal Body

The seventh level extends from two and one-half, to three and one-half feet from the body. It is the mental level of the spiritual plane. By raising our consciousness to the seventh level, we know we are one with the Creator. The seventh layer is in the shape of an egg and is composed of tiny threads of gold. The outer part of the egg is strong and resilient just like an eggshell protecting a chick. This shimmering golden template level contains the power current that runs up and down the spine, and nourishes the whole body. Colored bands of light, known as the past life bands, are also found within the eggshell.

Comment: I wish I could see auras at will. I saw a shimmering effervescent blue around a lady's head once. I was sitting at a table in a restaurant sipping a glass of wine. I noticed a pretty blue light and thought: I must be seeing an aura. My God! I am seeing an aura! Of course the minute I became excited, and my brain waves clicked back into racing formation, I could no longer see the aura. How I envy people like Barbara Brennan!

AUTOMATIC WRITING

To do automatic writing, a person enters a light trance and writes without realizing what is being written. An entity or spirit guide/teacher guides the hand or hands (in the case of a typewriter). This can be applied to painting and music as well.

Ruth Montgomery's books are probably the best examples of automatic writing. She received many writings which came from her spirit guides. She began her writings using a pencil and paper, devoting fifteen minutes per day. When her guide, "Lily," took over the sessions, Ruth was told to "go to your typewriter." She did, and thereafter the automatic writing became automatic typewriting. Many books were written by Ruth Montgomery in this fashion.

Comment: I once tried automatic handwriting. I said a prayer of protection, and attempted it for several weeks. My pencil did seem to write of its own accord. I received some rather profound thoughts and supposedly had a guide named Ronnie. He used to sign off with a picture of himself. (*See* picture.)

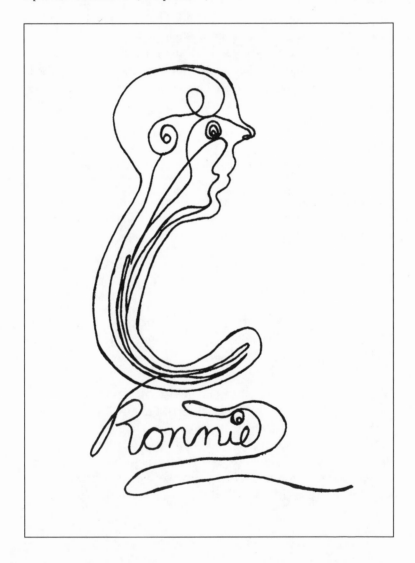

AVATAR

An *avatar* is a person whose soul is highly advanced or spiritually developed. This person has probably experienced many incarnations on the earth plane. Since this person is spiritually wise, he/she will exhibit compassion for humankind, spiritual insight, and unselfish service. The *avatar* understands life and its problems.

AWARENESS

Awareness is the state of being informed, knowing, and realizing. In the "New Age" sense, *awareness* transcends the limitations of time and space. We gather experiences in areas of being, which our senses cannot reach . . . then bring that experience back into our consciousness.

Awareness moves in all the dimensions of consciousness represented by memory, the senses, and the imagination.

Awareness is the bridge which leads consciousness from faith to knowledge and understanding.

B

Bermuda Triangle
Biofeedback
Blavatsky, Madam Helena
Brain Wave Frequencies
Buddhism

BERMUDA TRIANGLE

According to the channelings of Dr. Frank Alper, disappearances which have occurred in the area known as the Bermuda Triangle are a result of a powerful buildup of energy from damaged fire crystals from Atlantis. When the force field becomes strong enough, anything entering the field disintegrates and turns into pure energy. The energy from the crystals is only powerful enough to effect disintegration at certain times. Those individuals who have been caught in the force field have merely returned to spirit.

When the force field is not quite powerful enough to effect a total disintegration, it effects injuries. It could be compared to an individual receiving an overdose from a shock treatment. It is not enough to kill the person, but is enough to damage the brain structure causing insanity and other aberrations. Crew members from ships which seemingly vanished and returned under these particular circumstances, are found babbling away. The babbles they relate are: hallucinations, thoughts of fear, and manifestations of insanity. How unfortunate are these events.

BIOFEEDBACK

An electroencephalograph (E.E.G.) is a machine which shows the frequencies of brain waves. The E.E.G. machine consists of three basic parts: a set of electrodes, which are attached to the scalp of a person with a harmless paste; a brain wave amplifier; and a device for recording or displaying changes in the brain wave pattern. The recording device consists of a row of inked pens pressing against a continuously unwinding roll of graph paper.

These paper charts show that the brain has alpha, beta, theta, and delta waves. These waves are recorded in cycles per second (c.p.s.):

Alpha: 14 c.p.s. and up . . . associated with normal waking
exercises.

Beta: 7-14 c.p.s. . . . associated with a passive, relaxed state.

Theta: 4-7 c.p.s. . . . associated with creativity and hallucinations.

Delta: .5-4 c.p.s. . . . associated with sleep.

Biofeedback consists of a circuitry which translates the occurrence of alpha waves, as measured by the E.E.G. machine, into a tone. By using biofeedback, a subject can learn to produce alpha waves at will.

Biofeedback training may be the quick route to controlling your state of health, happiness, and well-being—as opposed to years of meditative techniques and training.

Comment: I once had an electroencephalogram done in London, Ontario to check out some dizzy spells. The neurosurgeon told me the brain emits enough electrical energy to light up a twenty-five watt bulb. Amazing!

BLAVATSKY, MADAM HELENA

Madam Blavatsky was the founder of the Theosophist Society. She was born in Russia in 1831. She married in her teens, but left her husband and started travelling to Turkey, Egypt, Greece, Canada, the U.S.A., South America, India, and Tibet. During her travels, she studied the religions of the countries through which she passed. She was especially affected by the mysticism of India and Tibet. Madam Blavatsky returned to America in 1873 where she founded the Theosophist Society with the help of Colonel H. S. Olcott and William Judge.

Madam Blavatsky died while setting up a London headquarters for the society in 1891. (*See* THEOSOPHY.)

BRAIN WAVE FREQUENCIES

Beta (β) Beta is the fastest level. Its frequency is between 14-21 cycles per second. At this level the mind focuses on the five physical senses as well as time, space, logic, reason and concrete objects. It is our outer consciousness, our waking state. It is like our fourth gear.

Alpha (α) Alpha is the next (slower) range of vibrations (7-14 c.p.s.). It is where intuition, inspiration, and creativity originate. The mind is free from worries and frustrations. This is the inner consciousness. Time and space become limitless. We can attain this state during meditation. Alpha is like our third gear.

Theta (θ) Theta is a slower brain wave frequency (4-7 c.p.s.). This is where most people fall asleep. Control of heart-beat, bleeding, and digestion occur here. This is the area of deep meditation. Theta is like our second gear.

Delta (Δ) Delta is the slowest brain wave frequency of all. (.5-4 c.p.s.) This area dominates in periods of very deep sleep, coma, or unconsciousness. Here the body repairs itself. Delta is like our first gear.

In-depth studies suggest that people using the slower rhythms of the brain increase their ability to: achieve desired goals; maintain positive attitudes; concentrate better; learn and recall better; and maximize their intuition. Also, greater control of blood pressure, muscle tension, and digestion can be achieved.

Healing occurs at several times the normally expected rate. Effective and constructive control of the mind can lead to psycho-somatic *health* rather than psychosomatic disease. The use of our inner levels triggers intuitive powers and makes problem solving easy by eliminating the guesswork. When one meditates, a person goes through these four major ranges of brain wave frequencies. It has been suggested that: one can overcome insomnia, control their weight, stop smoking, increase their productivity, utilize the intuitive powers, and gain greater peace of mind.

BUDDHISM

Buddhism is one of the great religions of the world. It originated in India twenty-five hundred years ago, but had its greatest influence in China, Japan, Tibet, Sri Lanka and Southeast Asia.

Like Hinduism, Buddhism shares the belief that human beings live many times on the earth plane. (*See* REINCARNATION.)

Buddhism stems from a single founder, Gautama Siddhartha, *the Buddha*. The *Buddha* is a title, meaning the Enlightened or Awakened One, and represents the ultimate goal, the realization of our own primordial nature. His teachings are known to Buddhists as the *Dharma*. *Dharma* is an untranslatable Sanskrit word with over ten meanings, embracing the ideas of truth, law, doctrine, and "what is right and proper." The *Sangha* is the community of Buddhist practitioners who have a common view and purpose.

There are three main evolutions within Buddhism: Hinayana (Theravada), Mahayana, and Vajrayana, representing the outer, inner, and "secret" or mystical teachings.

Theravada devotees revere the personality of the Buddha, his teachings, and the order he founded. They maintain that the ideal Buddhist is a faithful follower of the Eightfold Path, which involves Right Views, Right Morality, Right Motive, Right Speech, Right Action, Right Livelihood, Right Effort and Right Concentration.

Mahayana Buddhists regard the Buddha as one of many who have appeared. They hold that the ideal Buddhist is a compassionate *Bodhisattva*, one committed to becoming a Buddha through the Six Virtues: generosity, morality, patience, vigor, meditative awareness and non-dualistic wisdom.

The Buddha's original teachings were the Four Noble Truths: that there is suffering; ignorance is the cause of suffering; there is an end to suffering; and that there is a way to end suffering—by realizing the timeless nature of mind. Mind in its essence is radiant awareness. This enlightenment is attained through meditative experience which transcends thought and allows the mind to rest in a state of tranquil but alert awareness.

Vajrayana Tibetan Buddhism, or the Diamond Way, represents the esoteric teachings transmitted directly from the teacher to the advanced practitioner. The transmission may occur by words, actions, or mind-to-mind transference. These teachings involve the flow of subtle energy and the development of the "light" body.

Buddhist monks live in communities where the individual monk owns little or nothing. Local people support the monks in their monasteries with food and many other necessities. The monks, in turn, supply the community with spiritual and social services.

The Mahayana Buddhist believes that Maitreya, the Loving One, another reincarnation of the Buddha, is still to come in the future. The world in this time will be more beautiful and fruitful than now. Crops will grow by themselves, without labor. Every good Buddhist will be reborn then, and the human race will be much taller and stronger than today, and live much longer. Everyone will be honest and good, happy and prosperous. Crime and wrongdoing will no longer be contemplated. When Maitreya appears, everyone will attain enlightenment through his teaching. (Also *see* ZEN BUDDHISM.)

Comment: A teaching of Gautama Buddha states: "Be ye a refuge unto yourselves. Betake yourselves to no external refuge. Hold fast to the Truth as a lamp. Look not for refuge to anyone besides yourselves."

It seems to me that I have heard that song before.

C

Cayce, Edgar
Chakras
Channeling
Chanting
Chi
Chi Gong
Circles
Clairaudience
Clairsentience
Clairvoyance
Cosmic Consciousness
Course in Miracles, A
Cross
Crystals
Crystal Gazing

CAYCE, EDGAR

Edgar Cayce was a real pioneer for the New Age movement. It was more than twenty-five years ago that Cayce gave his first reading—a discourse about his own health, from a trance, or extended state of consciousness.

Cayce died in 1945, leaving behind volumes of information ranging from prehistory to predicted earth changes. All of the information emanated from his unconscious mind.

Most or his work, however, dealt with the human body, its illnesses, its nature, and its healing capabilities. Out of the 14,879 readings that are recorded and indexed in the library of the Association For Research and Enlightenment in Virginia Beach, Virginia, 8,968 were given for individuals who were concerned about their physical welfare.

Cayce's approach to health and healing can best be termed "holistic"—for, over and over again, while in his sleeping state, Cayce saw the human being as a whole entity in time and space. We are composed of mind, body, and spirit. Cayce felt the spirit is life, the mind acted as the builder, and the physical was the result.

Cayce saw man as a traveller in time and space, a stranger on earth, having his origin and destiny in the spiritual realms. Each of us is an eternal being, having existed in a form that is self-conscious prior to birth, and continues that existence when the physical body dies.

Because the physical is our present state of existence, Cayce directed most of his suggestions about healing toward the physical body. The process we go through in being healed of our physical and mental disabilities is, according to Cayce, an adventure in the consciousness.

CHAKRAS

Translated from the Hindi, *Chakras* means "wheels of energy." There are seven primary chakras or vortices in the human body, where we exchange a form of energy. When all seven chakras are in correct balance and alignment, we enjoy good health.

First Chakra (Root Chakra) The base or root chakra, or grounding chakra, is located at the base of the spine. It is perceived as the color red. The root chakra is associated with the adrenal gland (fight or flight) and governs the kidneys and spinal column. It is the center through which one understands the physical dimension.

Second Chakra The second chakra is located in the reproductive organs. It is perceived as the color orange. It governs one's creative attitudes in sex, reproduction, and relationships.

Third Chakra The third chakra is located in the solar plexus and is perceived as the color yellow. It is associated with emotional issues, and the pancreas. It governs the liver, spleen, stomach, gall bladder, and certain aspects of the nervous system.

A sobbing cry will massage the solar plexus reestablishing balance from an emotional overload.

Fourth Chakra (Heart Chakra) The fourth chakra is located at the heart. It is perceived as the color green. It is associated with the thymus gland. It governs the heart, blood circulatory system, and influences the immune and endocrine systems. It is through the heart chakra we "fall in love."

Fifth Chakra (Throat Chakra) The fifth chakra is located at the throat. It is perceived as the color blue. It is the center for self-expression and communication. It is associated with the thyroid gland and governs the lungs, vocal cords, bronchial tubes, and metabolism.

Sixth Chakra (Third Eye Chakra) The sixth chakra is located in the center of the forehead. It is seen as the color indigo (a combination of red and blue). It is the center through which we consider our spiritual nature. It is associated with the pituitary gland. It governs the lower brain and nervous system, the ears, the nose, and the left eye, known as the "eye of personality."

Seventh Chakra (Crown Chakra) The seventh chakra is located at the top of the head. Its color is violet, or sometimes the combination of all colors: white light. It is associated with the pineal gland. It is the center through which one may ultimately reach the feeling of *oneness* with God. The seventh center governs the upper brain and right eye.

CHANNELING

Channeling is not a new phenomenon. Its roots go back to Biblical days and earlier. Only recently has this age-old art gained widespread popularity. Now, literally thousands are learning how to access wisdom and information from a variety of sources.

Channeling, then, is a method of communication from some other level or dimension of reality to the conscious mind of the channel. The source of the information received includes: spirits of the deceased, the higher Self, the Universal Mind, space beings and higher guides and teachers.

The "channel" acts as a vessel or instrument which "tunes in" to the superconscious level of information. The channel can partially or totally set aside waking consciousness, to allow the information to flow. When the consciousness is totally set aside, a scribe, or tape recorder must be used so the channel can review the material in a wakeful state.

Jane Roberts is a trance channel who gave us the "Seth" material. This material originated in the 1960s. Findhorn, and the cooperation established between channels and the beings of the

Nature World, was a product of the '60s. "A Course In Miracles" which also came out in the '60s, was channeled material as well.

A very popular channel today is J.Z. Knight. She channels an entity that calls itself "Ramtha the Enlightened One." Ramtha claims to have been incarnated 35,000 years ago as a spiritual and political leader known as "The Ram" who came from Lemuria into what is now India. J.Z. Knight goes into a deep trance, and leaves her body to allow Ramtha to come through. Ramtha then uses the instrument (J.Z. Knight) to walk around, lecture, answer questions, and give out hugs.

Comment: I once attended an "Evening With Ramtha" in Burbaby B.C. Since I am from Ontario, the chance to view J.Z. Knight and the phenomenon of "Ramtha" was very intriguing for me. Wesley (my partner), and I took a room at the particular hotel where the event was held, so that we could go early and obtain a front-row seat. We went down to the hall approximately two hours prior to the lecture and were directed to line up in a waiting area outside the hall.

There was certainly a mixture of people waiting in the line-up. I enjoyed observing them as they each made their way to their place in the ever growing line. There were so many people in fact, that the line curved like a crazy snake. I was glad I was standing in the first section. Then the doors were opened and people funneled through the gap like a human stampede. Everyone who had arrived late, went through the doors first, and those who had waited patiently for hours, were the last to go through the doors. We obviously got the poorest of seats.

(Isn't there something in the Bible about "the first shall be last, and the last shall be first?")

I still have mixed feelings about that whole affair.

If you want to learn to channel, there are many books on the subject and courses to take. You will more than likely become what they call a "conscious channel." That means that you will remember the information that you receive. However, it is a good idea to keep a daily journal, because your impressions will fade very quickly.

I have attempted to channel with some success at times. (It is by no means as easy as I was led to believe.) One time stands out in my mind: I was about to "sign off" when I saw a flash of white light and I heard the words (inner hearing): "Go my child. Walk in the light . . . and KNOW that there are no foundations for your fears."

CHANTING

Chanting has been used over the centuries to help elevate your vibrations. Some people have their own mantra which they chant; others simply use the word "OM."

Musical chanting stimulates the flow of your vibrations and energizes them for you. Each color of the chakra system resonates to its corresponding level of consciousness as well as to its tone on the scale. Therefore, when meditating on a chakra color, you can augment the meditation by humming the corresponding note.

Chakra one . . . red . . . note C
Chakra two . . . orange . . . note D
Chakra three . . . yellow . . . note E
Chakra four . . . green . . . F
Chakra five . . . blue . . . G
Chakra six . . . indigo . . . A
Chakra seven . . . violet . . . B

"Om" can also be chanted with each color for a good meditative technique.

Harsh sounds affect our minds and bodies, and spirits (moods) in a detrimental way. Beautiful music, and the peaceful, rhythmic sounds of nature nourish us. Sound therapy can help you feel more peaceful, which in turn can make you feel more healthy. The Atlanteans used specific chants for various purposes.

CHI

Chi is the life force, or vital energy, and is said to flow through a system of channels in the body. Chinese medicine believes that when the flow of Chi is disturbed, illness results (*see* LIFE FORCE).

CHI GONG (QI GONG)

Chi gong, pronounced chi gung, is an ancient Chinese practice for generating the vital energy (Chi). The passive form deals with meditative practices, and the active form is a series of physical exercises that move the Chi.

CIRCLES

Because it has no beginning and no end, a *circle* has come to represent eternity and infinity. Circle shapes are used for development classes and healing sessions, known as "healing circles."

Anyone can participate in a development circle or a healing circle. If you are new to the concept, then the Spiritualist Church might be a good place to begin. They teach a few basic rules and routines which are very helpful to the beginner. They say a prayer of protection at the beginning of each session, and they have the knowledge to deal with any spiritual phenomena, should they occur.

Comment: I used to sit for spiritual development in the Hope Memorial Spiritualist Church in Brantford Ontario. The first year I sat, I saw nothing. I heard nothing. I felt nothing. It was very frustrating. Other members would see colors, see spirit, hear spirit, and occasionally someone would trance. I used to ask them if they saw spirit with their eyes open or their eyes shut. In fact, I asked that question so often, it became a joke.

Some years later, after taking several courses on meditation and human awareness, I decided to sit in Brantford again. I took a teacher friend with me so I would not have to drive the hour long trip alone. During the years I was away, the circle had really progressed, including the reverend of the church. She had learned to trance (or channel), and did so this particular evening. A North American Indian came through that night . . . war dance and all. When the medium's feet came to a halt, a very loud voice bellowed into the black-dark room . . . "HOW!"

I thought my friend, who was new to all this, was going to pass out right there on the spot. She was frightened by this sudden manifestation. There were many eventful evenings after that. One night an Oriental lady came through the medium, speaking only in her native tongue. We had to teach her English before we gleaned much from those sessions. Another night, a lady who had just passed over, came through. She had observed her own funeral preparations. She was most frightened, and did not want to leave. We had to reassure her, teach her to look toward "the light," and explain that she was now on the spirit side of life, before she would leave.

CLAIRAUDIENCE

Clairaudience is a form of very acute psychic hearing. The sensitive or medium, may feel as if somebody is speaking in whole sentences which arrive so rapidly the brain cannot register the meaning. The medium may have to send out the thought to "slow down" or "please repeat." In the beginning, it may be difficult for the sensitive to discern whether the audio impressions are arising from the medium's own mind or whether they "arrive" under spirit influence. Practice single, clearly formed questions; and the sending of loving affection to the spirit realms will assist clairaudient communications.

Comment: One evening I was attempting to give readings for a group of ladies. They were aware that I am a novice, but we all agreed it would be a lot of fun. For one lady, I could distinctly hear a calliope. When I told her this, she wanted to know what a calliope was. I explained that it was an old-fashioned steam instrument. When the player released steam from certain valves, he could actually play a melody. "Oh!" She exclaimed. A "_____." (She used a foreign word which I did not understand.) It turned out that one of her fondest memories was visiting her Grandma's house (in Holland) at the age of seven. The neighbor had a calliope and used to bring it over and play songs for her.

CLAIRSENTIENCE

If clairaudience is a form of psychic hearing, then *clairsentience* is a form of psychic smelling, tasting, or feeling something or some-one.

Comment: A friend of mine who used to sit in development classes with me could always tell when her grandmother (deceased) was around by the smell in the air. Her grandmother had been in the habit of using a particular scented soap . . . so when this aroma wafted through the air, my friend would invariably say, "I smell Grandma."

I had hired a young lad to look after my dalmatian dog while I was away for six months. Upon my return, I learned that "Blue" had developed a small growth on her hind leg. The veterinarian who had doctored Blue all of her eleven years, since she was a puppy, advised me to have the dog put to sleep. I asked the young lad to please take the dog to the vet for me and I declined seeing my old friend. I did not want to see her after such a long absence, since I was sure Blue would recognize me and I wasn't at all sure I would have the courage to take my old friend to the vet. I didn't want to know the exact day she would be going . . . knowing that Doctor White would simply send me a bill. Some days later, I could suddenly smell the dog as clearly as if she had walked into the room. The odor was distinctly her "doggie odor." "I guess Blue is in doggie heaven," I remarked. "I smell the dog." Two days later, the bill from Dr. White arrived in the mail. Does that mean that animals have souls? I would like to think so.

CLAIRVOYANCE

Clairvoyance is "seeing" with the inner eye. At first it is difficult
to separate clairvoyance from a heightened imagination. Some mediums do see spirit forms as solid objects, but it is necessary for
mediums to know that the center of psychic vision is not in the
physical eye, but within the forehead. What is "seen" may appear to
be superimposed upon a solid object, or "seen" when the physical
eyes are closed.

Sometimes clairvoyant vision will consist of a complete figure
or face of a person; or it may be a nebulous form hidden in a cloudy
substance. Sometimes it consists of brightly-colored symbols. The
onset of the opening of clairvoyant vision is frequently recognized
by swirling clouds of delicate colors within the head of the sitter. To
distinguish between imagination and inward consciousness (psychic
impressions), take note how the pictures are formed. In imaginary
pictures, the thinker visualizes the picture before it is seen—but if
the image is of psychic origin, it is seen first, and then thought about.
Indeed, the medium is often surprised by the fact that he/she has seen
something which is so unexpected. It is a good idea to keep a
notebook and record any clairvoyant impressions. Mediums have
varying lengths of time over which their visions can extend. These
can range from two days, to two weeks, to twenty years. By keeping
a notebook, the symbolism will also become clear.

Comment: The most vivid clairvoyant impression I ever received
is probably that of SNOW-FLY.

Wesley and I were travelling through northern Ontario, approaching the turn-off for Manitoulin Island. We had motored
through several Indian Reserves and I had noticed a couple of signs
advertising native art. In my mind, I had pictured their very stylized
form of art, and thus had no desire to stop.

"Why don't you meditate," Wesley said. "This is supposed to
be a power center."

I was bored from travelling for three days, so agreed to give it
a try. I began visualizing my colors from red to violet, which is my

particular meditative technique. When I reached the color yellow, a North American Indian suddenly stepped in. Since I was not through visualizing my colors, I told him he would have to wait—besides, I was not sure he wasn't just a figment of my imagination. When I finished, I mentally said: "O.K. You may speak now."

Well, speak he did! He ripped up one side of me and down the other. He was a "CHIEF," and not accustomed to waiting. He gave me proper shit. This was no figment of my imagination!

"Who you think you are? What make you think you no like our art? You like our country; you like our nature; what make you think you NO LIKE OUR ART?"

I told him I was very sorry for the attitude I had taken and promised to stop in, on my way back through. I asked him if he would show himself to me. The weathered face of an old native chief came into focus . . . reminding me of some postcards I had seen.

"What is your name?" I asked mentally. This seemed more difficult for him to convey. Maybe he'd used up a lot of energy yelling at me.

At first I saw snow swirling around—flying through the air.

Snowflake?

Next he showed me a trout fly like the ones you use for fly fishing.

Snowfly?

This seemed to be the answer. Chief Snowfly seemed to have mellowed out and soon departed. I was intrigued. No spirit had ever yelled at me before.

Later, I went to a library and looked up the word "snowfly" in the reference section. To my surprise, there is indeed, a tiny insect called a *snowfly* which jumps about in the snow. Chief Snowfly may have been named after a tiny bug, but there was nothing small about his personality. He was a powerful entity.

By the way, I now own two pieces of native art . . . a blue heron, and another titled "Loon Majesty."

COSMIC CONSCIOUSNESS

Cosmic consciousness radiates from God. It pervades all space and all things. It knows all past, present, and future . . . for it is all. Through meditation and study, we can attune ourselves with the Cosmic Consciousness, to become illuminated, or enlightened.

COURSE IN MIRACLES, A

A *Course in Miracles* is a set of three books, published by the Foundation for Inner Peace, which has evolved for many people into a home-study course augmented by study groups. This highly evolved treatise on inner spirituality was channeled from the other side and aims at finding God's peace within and learning the principles of love, healing, and miracles.

CROSS

The use of the *cross* as a symbol of goodness pre-dates Christianity. It was originally a symbol of fertility representing the union of the phallic male (the upright member) and the receptive female (the cross member). The center of the cross marks infinity because it is the meeting place of the four cardinal points of the compass to which the arms point. Some people visualize the cross as a symbol of protection. There are hundreds of different types of crosses. More than fifty different designs are recognized by the Anglican Church alone. (*See* illustrations below.)

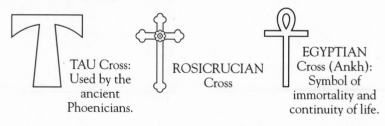

TAU Cross: Used by the ancient Phoenicians.

ROSICRUCIAN Cross

EGYPTIAN Cross (Ankh): Symbol of immortality and continuity of life.

CRYSTALS

The name "crystal" comes from a Greek word meaning *clear ice* or *frozen water.*

Natural quartz crystals are formed from the elements silicon and water through a long process involving pressure and heat. The finest crystals are being mined in Arkansas, Herkimer, N.Y., Mexico, and Brazil.

Their natural formation consists of six sides or faces with a point on one end, and sometimes two ends. A crystal with a point on both ends is referred to as "double-terminated."

Quartz crystals can be clear or colored. Included in the quartz family are: amethyst (purple), blue quartz, rose quartz, citrine quartz (various shades of yellow), green quartz, rutilated quartz (streaked with gold and copper fibers), and quartz with black, blue or green tourmaline rods inside.

Energy, in the form of vibration, is projected from each crystal. A one-half inch crystal projects a field of around three feet.

Comment: If the Atlanteans used crystals which were 25 feet tall and 10 feet in diameter, I wonder how far their energy field projected?

Crystals are used in radio and television broadcasting, but New Age thinkers are more concerned with how they can use crystals on a more personal level.

It is felt that crystals can assist in healings, meditations, affirmations, psychic abilities, and astral travels.

You can charge your crystal by: putting it in sunlight, holding it under a waterfall, or leaving it outside in the wind. Some people leave their crystals outside over night to charge them with the feminine moon energy. It is best to charge each crystal with one type of energy, then wrap it up in a natural fibre until you would like to use it.

When choosing a crystal, take the one which seems irresistible, that intuitively feels right to you.

Generally, crystals which you have set aside for a specific use, should not be handled by others. It is felt that working with quartz crystals, changes or manipulates the vibrations on a subtle, non-physical level to affect the related vibrations on a physical level. Quartz crystals are chosen because they have extremely high and exact rates of vibration which will resonate in harmony with any vibration with which it is brought into contact.

Because all manifestation of being is essentially vibration, quartz crystals can be used to: modify thoughts, emotions, and our physical bodies. Negative emotions can be changed to positive; disharmony transformed to harmony; bodies energized or healed.

Crystals in the hands of trained workers, can create miracles.

Comment: I own some crystals, but I do not work with them at this point in time. I particularly like the "feel" of my amazonite (green) crystal, which I found at a mine in northern Ontario.

A friend of mine has a smokey quartz crystal approximately six inches long and two inches wide. I admired it, so she gave it to me to hold. I placed it in my left hand, with the point aiming up my arm. We walked around the house chatting, while I held the crystal. Suddenly, I felt very dizzy, as though I could pass out. I asked my friend if the crystal had anything to do with my sensations. She immediately snatched the crystal from my hand and put it away. The feeling of dizziness soon cleared away. Obviously the crystal had something to do with it. I can't explain it—but I know I felt it. My friend never did comment.

One day Wesley and I stopped at a rock shop in British Columbia. I wanted to purchase some small jade carvings of bears. As we looked around the shop, we noticed numerous rocks and crystals. Our attention was drawn to several clusters of quartz crystals. The lady who owned the shop was a dear, white-haired elf of a person. She had to be nearing her eightieth birthday, and might have weighed ninety-eight pounds, soaking wet.

Wesley said to me, "Put your hand over these crystals. What do you feel?" I was just beginning to be able to discern some differences between certain crystals and stones. The quartz cluster felt relatively cool. Nothing doing, but try another one. This quartz cluster had numerous miniature crystals as well as the three or four larger, more defined ones. To my amazement, this cluster felt very much warmer, when I placed my hand slightly above the grouping. The wee lady looked at us through her spectacles as though either she, or we, had lost our minds. Curious however, she too, placed her hand over the clusters in turn. Suddenly a smile broke over her face. She also felt the warmth emanating from the second cluster of crystals.

"Hmmmm," she grinned, "it must be all the little babies."

CRYSTAL GAZING

Gazing into a crystal ball for visions of the past, present, and future, is a very ancient pastime. It dates back as far as the Greeks and is found in ancient civilizations throughout the world.

Beryl crystal is the most popular crystal used by a medium of "crystal-gazing."

The ball acts as a kind of primitive television screen for the clairvoyant who consults it. Symbols, pictures, or places appear, which must be interpreted.

When you find your crystal begins to look dull or cloudy, with small pin points of light glittering like stars, you know that you are beginning to obtain crystalline vision. The crystal will clear and visions will manifest.

Comment:

Looking into a glass of water will give you a similar focal point with a lot less expense.

I once attended a day-long seminar in Toronto Ontario. The lecturer guaranteed you could do "readings" by the end of the day—or you got your money back. There were various exercises he put us through during the day, which I won't go into, but the culmination of the day (for me), was when we were directed to gaze into a glass of water, and observe a message for the person sitting next to us. "Sure," I thought, "I sat in classes for a whole year in Brantford . . .

and never saw a thing. This man wants me to look into a glass of water and give a message to someone else?" I looked . . . and lo and behold, there in my glass of water, were two little stick figures representing two little girls. You know, the kind four- to seven-year-old children draw? A circle for the head; two dots for the eyes; a smiley face; sticks for arms and legs? My two figures wore a triangle for a dress. They looked exactly alike, so I assumed they were both girls, although I kept wanting to call one a little boy. Talk about surprised; I think you could have knocked me over with a feather! I turned to the lady sitting next to me.

"Do you have a set of twins?" I asked.

"Yes," she answered.

"Girls?"

"Yes," she nodded again.

"I see two stick figures of little girls, but I keep wanting to call one a little boy."

"That's funny," she exclaimed. "My husband and I were just discussing the twins this morning . . . and how one is such a tomboy, and should have been a boy."

D

Dancing
Development
Disease (Dis-ease)
Divination
Divine Intelligence
Dowsing
Dreams
Drumming
Dzog Chen

DANCING

The practice of dancing during magical rites remains an essential ingredient of many religious ceremonies in Africa, and in the East even today.

North American native Indians also use ceremonial dances.

The purpose of dancing seems to be twofold. It pleases the gods, and releases the emotions of the dancers. Some dancers work themselves into a frenzy, eventually passing into a semi-conscious, trance-like state.

Whirling dervishes are members of any of various Moslem orders. Their whirling dances and howling are part of their religious acts.

The "Shakers" trembled from head to foot in religious transports of ecstasy. In the mid-eighteen hundreds approximately 4,000 Shakers inhabited eighteen communities from Maine to Kentucky. Their belief in a celibate life probably contributed to their decline of later years.

Dancing evolved into marches, which died out by the 1930's. Earlier, with a revival of spiritualism, members received divinely inspired "gifts" of dance, song, or drawings.

Many dances were connected with the weather and nature. Primitive tribes danced to bring rain and ensure fertility of the soil.

Spiritual seekers today are returning to the dance as a means with which to center themselves, to create balance, and assist their meditations.

Comment: Some of my happiest memories are when the children and I made up our own dances at the school where I taught. In fact, the children were better at it than I was. (I don't know why that should surprise me.) We always felt better after we danced.

DEVELOPMENT

In the new age context, *development* means spiritual progression, spiritual awareness, and a growth of one's spiritual talents.

Learning to develop your spiritual talents is somewhat like learning to play the piano. Potentially, all of us have a latent gift for playing the piano. Some will choose to develop those skills and take piano lessons. Some of us have a natural gift, and can play anything without lessons. Some people are not interested in playing at all. If you can relate your spiritual progression to taking piano lessons, it may help.

Most people have to take piano lessons for years, before they become proficient at it. Most people have to practice meditation for years before they become proficient at that.

I am one of those plodders. Nothing comes easy. I only have grade eight piano; and my meditation skills are still mediocre after years of working at it. I cannot channel a specific guide, or tune into a specific entity. My contacts are very hodge-podge—hit and miss. Many times I pick up nothing at all during a meditation session.

I tell you this so you, my reader, will not become discouraged if you are just beginning your path of spiritual progression. So many books try to state how easy all this is. Well . . . it isn't! At least for some of us. If you persevere, you will harvest enough spiritual gems to keep you going. One of my most precious gems, came to me the night I was able to contact my dad, who is on the "other side."

As I lay in bed one late August evening, I decided to try a meditation. Suddenly, dad came in. He said he was the one who told me to wash the rug the other night, when I thought it was Wes talking. I asked for a stronger connection since I didn't want to think it might be my imagination. He sang a number of songs to me which included: "If I Were the Only Boy In the World," "Shanty Town," "Sweetheart of Sigma Chi," "My Ideal," and some of his other favorites. Then he picked up his fiddle and played "Five Foot Two" and "Sweet Georgia Brown." (Dad always played these two songs when he was on the earth plane.) He would have gone on and on, so I stopped him, so we could talk. I told him I'd heard he had a little sleep when he first went over. He said he had, and then awakened to find out "by damned," if he wasn't still alive. Then he apologized for saying the word "damned." He said for someone (meaning myself) who always talked about life after death—that I was sure hard to get through to. I explained that it's pretty difficult when you're still in the physical. Then he showed me a picture of himself of when he and mom were both young. I calculated that it was taken around the time I was born. He showed me the old living room at the farmhouse where I grew up. There was an old rocking chair; mom was sitting, rocking a baby; and I was the baby. The old furnace grate was still there. Then dad said, "Daddy's little girl." Mom seemed shy and wouldn't talk—but she was all giggly, like a young girl when dad teased her. I heard her say, "Oh Kenneth!" I asked dad how he felt about Warren (my brother), selling the old farmhouse. Dad reflected for a moment, then said, "I would kind of hate to see it go—but we all have to say goodbye to physical attachments sooner or later."

I wondered if he ever saw Alan (my late husband who died of a brain tumor in 1985).

"Not too often. We never had much in common. We see Clark from time to time." I got the impression that dad saw Clark due to their lodge affiliation.

"So," I asked, "What are you doing to keep yourself busy?"

"Growing tomatoes."

"Growing tomatoes! Whatever for?" Dad had grown many fields of tomatoes while on the earth plane. I couldn't imagine in God's green earth, why he would want to grow tomatoes as a pastime over there. I assume dad picked up that thought wave because he immediately said, "You can do anything you want to over here . . . and I'm growing tomatoes."

"What is mom doing?" I asked.

"She's knitting. She's so glad to be able to see again, that she's knitting everything in sight." (Mom had lost so much of her eyesight in her latter years, she could no longer enjoy her knitting.)

"Do you know Tulma?" I asked. (Tulma is one of my guides.)

"He's the one who arranged to bring me here. He's on a much higher plane. Guess I'd better turn you over to him." Dad and I both agreed to talk again.

The vibrations shifted and Tulma came in. Tulma describes himself as a "being of light" and visits quite regularly. The vibrations were much calmer by comparison, not as agitated. He began with "I am Tulma." I thanked him for arranging my visit with dad and told him that he (Tulma) and I would talk again tomorrow morning. Instead of the usual farewell of: "Go my child, and walk in the light" . . . Tulma said:

"Good night. Sleep tight.

Don't let the bed-bugs bite.

But if they do . . .

Turn on the light."

Now do you see why I call this one of my personal gems?

DISEASE (Dis-ease)

New age thinkers are beginning to look at disease as really "dis-ease." When there is a general disturbance of the harmonious constructive process of the living, creative cells—we are in a state of "dis-ease."

The logical procedure for restoring health, is to help nature, by ending the cause of the disturbance when it is known. Proper breathing, proper eating, proper exercise, enough sleep, and positive thinking are the first essentials in helping nature remove the inter-ference.

Holistic health practitioners can help steer us down the path to health. They can help us become aware that we are indeed a complex being, consisting of much more than just the physical body. Our inner, divine spark has supreme wisdom. We can use it to guide our daily life, our health, and our growth.

Health is complete balance at all levels. We create our health or disease, according to our beliefs. Pain may be an education of the soul. Ask yourself what your body is trying to tell you. When you remember who you are, the process for healing can begin. Ultimately, we must learn to take responsibility for our own health or "dis-ease."

DIVINATION

Divination is the practice of asking an outside force to decide our future actions.

Almost any aid can be used because the skill lies in interpreting the signs, not in the objects themselves.

Some methods of divination include: astrology, numerology, the tarot, palmistry, crystal gazing, psychometry, dream interpretation, runes, and channeling.

Comment: I think all of us would like to be able to see into the future, although I must admit, sometimes it's a blessing we can't. Some years ago, I visited a spiritualist camp in Cassadega Florida. I had read an article about Cassadega, so when my daughter and I flew to Florida to visit friends, I decided to go to Cassadega.

I had a reading done by a kind old gentleman while sitting inside a screened gazebo. The most outstanding thing he told me was that I would be living in a different geographical location by the year 1990. I had the reading done in 1986. Since I had lived my entire life (over forty years) in southern Ontario, I very much doubted his prediction. However, I wrote it down. As I sit writing . . . it is now 1991—and I am in British Columbia in my vacation home which I purchased in 1988. Amazing!

DIVINE INTELLIGENCE

Divine Intelligence is another way of saying Cosmic Consciousness or God Consciousness. It is part of the spiritual realms, and is there for us to draw upon when we need it for help of any nature;

whether it be for growth, health, or rescue from danger. Ask, and you will receive.

DOWSING

Dowsing is an age-old method of locating a desired spot by using (a) a forked stick, (b) L-shaped rods, or (c) a pendulum. The dowser may seek out underground water, minerals, buried artifacts, or power cable failures. At the key point, the "divining rod" twists in the hand. (A pendulum will start to twirl.)

The rod or pendulum serve to amplify bodily responses to subtle forces—probably magnetic. The human body functions as a magnetic detector. Tiny variations in the earth's magnetic field cause muscular twitches that result in a visible reaction in the rod or pendulum.

English dowser, Guy Underwood, found that "water lines" often converge at "knots" under sacred sites marked by churches or megalithic henges, where the "earth force" is strongest. (*See* VORTEX.)

Offshoots from main subterranean water lines (whorls) are called *positive* or *negative* nodes. Gnats and other insects hover above positive nodes, returning if blown away. Ants build nests here, and wild animals prefer to give birth at these locations. Negative nodes are favored by plants or trees like weeping willow, but adversely affect the health of people in houses ignorantly built over them. Mice placed in an enclosure half on and half off such a zone, will not sleep in it. Celery, cucumbers, onions and ash trees barely grow at all in such areas.

German dowser, Wilhelm de Boer suggested that the water-detecting organ involved in dowsing is the adrenal gland. Aluminum foil wound around the head above the ear, blocks the signals, as does a square patch of foil pasted on the forehead. De Boer was so sensitive, he could dowse different radio stations.

Expert dowsers can choose what they want to locate by tuning in on a precise signal, be it gold, water, or bodily remains.

T.C. Lethbridge, working with pendulums, discovered that pendulums can be tuned to respond to a particular object. He found (when seeking truffles) that a pendulum held on the end of a seventeen-inch cord reacted to truffles.

Map dowsing can be used to seek minerals or missing persons. A dowser moves the pendulum over a map until it reacts at a particular point. How it works is not fully understood, but one thing *is* generally accepted—*dowsing* DOES work.

Comment: You can make your own dowsing rod using two wire coat hangers. Cut off the curled ends and bend them straight. About one-third of the distance from the end of the wire, bend each wire 90°. When you have them bent, hold them in your hands by the short end, so the long end points out in front of you, and is level to the ground. Hold them lightly enough to allow them to turn freely. Mentally direct the rods to move when they detect an energy field.

I once attended a workshop where a gentleman operated an aurameter (*see* AURA) which is a refined form of dowsing rod. The gentleman would walk towards an individual holding the aurameter which would deflect away from the energy field when it reached the edge. The aurameter can be an excellent tool for showing changes in the human energy field when a healing has been done.

DREAMS

Everyone dreams, every night. The trick is remembering them.

In a sleep state, the astral body of the sleeper journeys into the astral planes seeking knowledge and guidance. With practice, these dreams or experiences can be remembered. Often, symbols are given which must be interpreted.

Good symbols promising wealth, love, happiness, and fulfillment of desires include: anchors, angels, auctions, bees, birds, bread, bride, butterflies, candles, castles, cherries, climbing, gold or silver coins, compasses, daisies, dancing, diamonds, eagles, fire, fish, flying, growing flowers, frogs, white horses, ladders, lobsters, nurses, oaks, orchards, parties, rainbows, ribbons, rice, saddles, scales, sheep, ships, shovels, spoons, stars, strawberries, sun, white swans, white teeth, toys, turkeys, vases of flowers, fresh vegetables, vineyards, violins, watches, woods, and yachts.

Some believe we are more alive in the dream state than when we are walking around in the physical dimension. If we are basically spiritual creatures, then perhaps the dream world is our normal habitat; and our material world the illusion.

Comment: Dreams have always fascinated me. I include a poem which I wrote some years ago.

Dreams

Our bodies, though they be earthly bound,
make cradles for our souls;
vessels for our thoughts profound . . .
and help us reach our goals.
Therefore, they often intermingle
from darkest depths, to heaven's gates;
back home, they each are single.
But where is home? And what is real?
The waking or the sleeping?
What we dream? Or what we feel?
The sowing; or the reaping?
These many questions fill my brain,
my mind, my soul, my heart.
I think perhaps I'll go insane . . .
if our souls must always part!
Each night we go to dreamland;
our souls give flight and soar
together, happy. Hand in hand
they fly from door to door
seeking answers to life's question

behind a door or gate—
but after every session, are forced to separate.
So we must be content to live apart,
and wait another meeting. Flesh can be
one flesh; our bodies will be spent,
but our souls, their mates are greeting.

DRUMMING

Playing drums in groups is a practice common to all indigenous cultures for ceremony, celebration, and the induction of altered states of consciousness.

DZOG CHEN

Dzog Chen, literally meaning "great perfection," is a view of reality taught by authentic, realized masters in Vajrayana Tibetan Buddhism. The object of the meditation is to recognize the nature of your own mind as inseparable from the Buddha-nature. The practice is designed to lead a student from the suffering, deluded state into a radiant awareness of empty clear space out of which pure compassion arises.

E

Earth-bound Spirit
Ectoplasm
Elementals
Emanation
Entity
Esotericism
E.S.P.
Essenes
Ether
Evolution
Evolved

EARTH-BOUND SPIRIT

An *earth-bound spirit* is what people generally refer to as a ghost. They are poor departed souls who are so ill prepared for the spiritual realms that they do not realize they have passed over the barrier we call death. Everything looks the same to them, but we cannot, as a rule, see them. The earth-bound spirit cannot figure out why people will not pay attention to them.

These souls often have emotional, or psychological attachments to places on the earth plane, and that is why they haunt particular places. In such cases, it is necessary to explain logically to them, that they have indeed departed from the physical realms, and that they now inhabit the spiritual realms. Explaining to them that they must look for the light, and be about their business, usually helps. If they realize they are not wanted particularly, in the house where they are causing some distress to the new inhabitants, these earth-bound spirits will generally leave. Be kind, understanding, and firm.

Some spiritualist churches have groups which deal solely (pardon the pun) with earth-bound spirits. These circles are known as "rescue circles."

ECTOPLASM

Ectoplasm is a cloudy, vaporous substance that flows from a physical medium's ears, nostrils, or mouth, which is then converted into a silky material. The visiting spirits are then able to clothe themselves with the ectoplasm in order to appear and converse with their friends; or give instruction to those seeking advice from the world of spirit. Such materializations where spirit appears in a semi-solid form, clothed in white drapery, and capable of speaking in the same language and tone of voice as during their earthly life time—are rare today.

Most mediums produce such a small amount of ectoplasm that it is not possible for a full materialization to take place. Spirit can use small amounts of ectoplasm to make a temporary larynx which they use to speak, and make their words audible to all listeners. This is known as "direct voice mediumship."

In transfiguration, the features of the medium temporarily disappear under a mask of ectoplasm in which the spirit faces appear instead of that of the medium.

When spirits use a small supply of ectoplasm to create a psychic photograph (a photograph on which a spirit face appears in addition to the normal details of the subject captured by the camera lens), you can be sure someone is present who possesses some degree of physical mediumship. Darkness is essential for physical mediumship.

ELEMENTALS

Elementals are the lowest form of spirits. These beings are able to manifest themselves on the physical plane by wrapping denser layers of matter around themselves.

These spirits are not enlightened and can be filled with mischief or evil intentions. Fear is an attractive force with regards to these spirits. If you are afraid of spirit contact, then you should leave it alone. There is a law which states: "Like attracts like." Design your life so that you will draw the kind of company you desire—both in the physical and the spiritual realms. Seek only the spiritual connection of the higher planes where wisdom and love abound. Seek to expand the God-consciousness within yourself. God's light is in every heart.

Comment: Robert Monroe, in his book *Journeys Out of the Body*, describes several meetings with what I believe to be elementals. He records these encounters from his astral travels.

During one astral trip he was attacked by something. It had no apparent personality, and the struggle was silent and terrifyingly fast.

The "thing" moved from nerve center to nerve center applying excruciating pressure. Robert fought back savagely and with desperation. When he realized he was out of the physical, he steered the fight towards his physical body, and dropped "back in."

On another astral trip, a little creature climbed onto his back. It was humanoid in form, but lacked human intelligence. When Mr. Monroe tried to pull the little rascal off his back, the little body stretched like rubber. Then another creature appeared. Mr. Monroe became extremely frightened. Then the creatures turned into a good facsimile of each of his two daughters. A deliberate camouflage on their parts to create emotional confusion. Eventually, a man showed up, picked up both of the little beings and rescued Robert.

Sometimes these elementals, or lower spirits, manifest through the Ouija Board. So . . . you better know what you are doing when it comes to communicating with the spirit realms.

EMANATION

An *emanation* is something that comes from something or someone. This term is often used in Tibetan Buddhism and other Eastern religions to describe a being who contains the essence of a particular saint who is born on earth to continue that being's spiritual mission or blessing.

ENTITY

The word *entity* is often used to refer to a spirit personality who manifests itself through some form of mediumship, meditation, or channeling. Often, we do not know their name, or why they appeared, but we do sense their personality. For this reason, most people simply refer to them as an "entity," unless the spiritual visitor wishes to further identify itself. Usually an entity makes itself felt or seen, in order to help us with a material problem or aid our spiritual growth.

Comment: Years ago when I sat in a development circle, we had an "entity" come to us on a regular basis. One person in the group acted as the channel. Whenever we wanted to ask a question, members of the group prefaced their query with "Entity, tell us . . ." We never did learn its name, nor does it really matter. Whenever we sat, we always said a prayer of protection, and asked for the "highest and the best." Our Entity was always most gracious—and on some occasions down right humorous.

ESOTERICISM

Esotericism means: "the living inner reality," that which is innate or indwelling.

A student of esotericism strives to understand his inner self, consequently an air of mystery shrouds the aspirant. Esoteric knowledge used to be considered beyond the understanding of most people. Thus only a chosen few, as an inner group of disciples or initiates, were labelled esoterics.

The knowledge obtained through esoteric studies often had to be kept secret in order to avoid persecution throughout various periods of history.

E.S.P.

E.S.P. stands for *extra sensory perception.* We have five basic senses, besides common sense. These include: seeing, hearing, tasting, smelling, and touching. When we "know" something without using one of the five senses, we are said to acquire that knowledge through E.S.P. It can apply to little things like knowing who is on the line when the phone rings, to big things such as avoiding a particular airplane flight, because you "know" the plane is going to crash. E.S.P. can cover the past, present, or future. All of us possess some E.S.P. If we learn to listen to it, our E.S.P. will seldom steer us in a wrong direction.

ESSENES

The *Essenes* were communities of white-robed spiritual seekers who lived in the deserts of the Holy Land around the time of Christ (250 B.C. to A.D. 100).

The community of Qumran existed before the time of Christ. It is supposed that the Essenes wrote the "Dead Sea Scrolls" which have been found in caves near the ruins of an ancient spiritual center outside of Haifa, Israel, near the old Qumran water hole. The discovery of the Dead Sea Scrolls in 1947 brought to new light the wisdom-teachings of the Essene communities that existed in the deserts of the Middle East.

These spiritual communities were dedicated to preserving the ancient teachings and to preparing the way for the new age of Pisces, when Christ energy would flood the world. The Essenes lived in simple harmony with all of nature, following the spiritual wisdom of their inner voices, which the Buddhists call "living one's dharma." Their spiritual practices allowed them to absorb and channel the vibrations and healing powers of the plants, the sun, and the four elements of earth, air, fire, and water—for their own nourishment and for the healing of the earth itself. We have much to learn from these simple folk.

The Essene teachings tell us that John the Baptist was an Essene master, and that he and other Essene teachers trained the initiate Jesus in the ancient wisdom during that twenty-year period of his life, about which the Bible is silent.

Essenes were committed to bringing their spiritual awareness into their daily life. They lived in colonies and opened their doors to any sect who came their way. They had a storehouse, common expenditures, common clothes, and common food. This was made possible by their practice of putting whatever they earned daily into a common fund, out of which the sick were supported when they could not work. The older members were objects of reverence and honor. Stewards were appointed to take care of their common affairs.

They did not change clothes or shoes until their own completely wore out. They had a barter system. Their day consisted of: morning prayers; labor until five in the afternoon; then assemblage in one place. They dressed in white veils, then they bathed their bodies in cold water. After this purification, they would go into the dining room where a baker provided loaves. The cook brought a single plate of one sort of food and set it before each one. It was unlawful to taste of the food before grace was said. The Essenes were peaceful and honest. They took great pains in studying the writings of the ancients and chose out of them what would be an advantage to their soul and body. Women were equal to men, so both men and women could join the Essenes.

They had a knowledge of medicine stones and herbal remedies. Ancient documents describe the Essenes as people who were masters of an even older wisdom of cosmology, astrology, herbal healing, and numerology. They could be used as models of holistic living for today's disconnected society.

Their love for one another and of the Spirit; their harmony with all living things; and their understanding of Universal Law, stand as timeless teachings for anyone seeking to re-attune to the subtle, natural spirituality that lies behind the fragmented theology of present-day religion.

The first small group of Jews who retreated to the desert in about 250 B.C. were followers of the ancient tradition of Melchizedek. This tradition told of a being who had appeared thousands of years prior, in a ball of fire, without mother or father. He was Melchizedek, the Teacher of Righteousness. He had to tell the world that our birthright gave us a direct connection to the Godhead; that God lived in our hearts, not in some high place available only to priests and kings. In those times, this was quite radical to say or believe.

Over the centuries, people forgot, and a class of priests and politicians inserted themselves between God and the people. If the people wanted to communicate with their God, they had to pay a priest to sacrifice an animal, and then maybe, just maybe, the priest could intercede for them with God. The followers of the Melchizedek tradition left the corruptions of these cities and established communities in the desert where they could reestablish their direct God-communication. They called themselves Essaie, and prepared themselves for the return of Messiah, who would manifest through the next Teacher of Righteousness.

As the first Essenes grew old, they realized that Messiah was not going to return in their lifetimes and therefore, they would have to reorganize their communities so that their lineage could continue the preparations for as long as it took. The Essene desert communities then became true villages, with families raising their young, in the consciousness of "preparing the way" for newness . . . for the change that was to come. The Dead Sea Scrolls tell us that each succeeding generation became more attuned, and that finally, babies were being born who already were conscious of their role in the bringing of this energy of Messiah. One such lineage was that of Elizabeth and her kinswoman Mary, in the community of Qumran, near Mount Carmel. The Scrolls indicate that Elizabeth gave birth to a conscious being who became known as the Daystar; who went into the wilderness to prepare for the eminent arrival of the Teacher of Righteousness. Was this Daystar, John the Baptist?

And then Mary gave birth to a son at Qumran who grew to become the Teacher of Righteousness. (The name *Jesus* is not mentioned in the Dead Sea Scrolls. However, with reference to the term "Jesus of Nazareth," it seems that *Nazarene* refers not so much to a place 2000 years ago, as it did to a spiritual belief—a particular way of living. It also appears that the term "Nazarini" and the term "Essene" meant the same thing.)

It is perhaps more than a coincidence that during the same years that our Bible tells us Jesus was "in the desert" (and it says no more), the scrolls tell that the Teacher of Righteousness was involved in a comprehensive educational process. He was first taken to every Essene community to learn from all the wise teachers therein. He was taken to India to learn the wisdom of ancient Vedic tradition, and then to Persia. After this, he was led to Egypt to study with the White Brotherhood. During the last few years of his training, the scrolls fall silent about his whereabouts. The thread is picked up by another ancient tradition, in the Celtic lands, now known as southern England.

Glastonbury, the mystical site of the Druid Chalice Well, and the spiral Tor mountain, was not always landlocked. Two thousand years ago it was the Island of Avalon. Celtic legend tells of two beings from the Holy Land: Joseph of Arimathea, and his nephew Jesus, sailing up the river to Avalon, teaching, learning, and bringing great joy. They left a gift . . . a white rose bush, that would only bloom in the midst of winter. (A cutting from a cutting, of that bush, still blooms through the Glastonbury snow each winter.) It was only after these far-flung teachings and initiations, that the son of the Essene Mary, became the receptacle of the energy of the Messiah, allowing the love of Agape to flow in the world, changing our human destiny forever.

ETHER

Ether is the state between energy and matter. Our physical bodies are a result of our etheric bodies. The etheric body is composed of tiny energy lines, similar to the lines on a television screen. It has the same structure as our physical body, including organs and anatomical parts. Our physical body is sort of draped over our etheric body and anchored into it.

Our etheric body is constantly in motion and appears as sparks of bluish-white light extending up to two inches beyond our physical body. (*See* AURAS.)

EVOLUTION

Evolution is the progressive growth and perfecting of our souls. As we strive onward and forward, toward perfection, our vibrational level is raised higher and higher.

EVOLVED

An *evolved* soul is one which has reincarnated many times and has reached a stage closer to perfection than the unevolved soul.

F

Fairies
Faith Healing
Feng Shui
Fire Walking
Flower Essences

FAIRIES

Dora van Gelder in her book, *The Real World of Fairies*, claims she can see fairies and describes them at great length. Here is a brief summary of some of the fairy folk. (I cannot see them.)

Fairies can range in size from that of a butterfly to several feet in height.

Angels or Devas are radiant beings of great intelligence who help guide nature by their understanding of the Divine Plan. They oversee the lesser fairies.

Air Fairies Air spirits who live at very high altitudes resemble great dragons with huge heads, long bodies, and a long tail. They are of low intelligence and never descend to the lower atmosphere.

Cloud fairies build cloud-forms and are particularly fond of sunsets and sunrises. Air fairies who are associated with the wind and storms are from four to five feet high. They are well proportioned, according to the human model. Their narrow faces are framed with streaming hair. They have the coloring of a silver birch with faint lights of blue and violet. They are fairly intelligent.

The most definite creatures of the airy kingdom are the sylphs. They have perfect human features and form. Their child-like faces are beautiful. They are surrounded by a mist and look like opals under sunlight. Their bodies are made of much finer stuff than of any other fairy. Their intelligence is far superior to other kinds of fairies, so it is easier to communicate with them. They can read our thoughts. Most sylphs are in service to angels, performing specific tasks, in an attitude of profound love. Sylphs also attend to human beings. They act as guardian angels to people. They are often found in hospitals, particularly near the dying. Their greatest joy is to assist children who have just passed over and feel lost and strange. Sylphs play with children and tell them wonderful "fairy" tales.

Earth Fairies Earth fairies consist of four main types and include both the surface and the underground. Tree fairies have a physical body, while common garden or woods fairies do not. Gnomes (associated with rocks) do not have physical bodies either.

A kind of earth fairy which is almost universal, is tiny (one to one-and-a-half feet), and is a golden brown or dark green color. Such fairies suggest a mouse to humans because of their rather long ears and general habit of hopping about. They are cheerful beings of low intelligence. They have two legs, but move somewhat like mice with quick, jerky movements. They are sociable creatures and live in communities. They inhabit the forest areas looking after the moss and the life forces of living things.

There are numerous garden fairies. Some look like candles, while a typical garden fairy looks quite human in appearance. He is between one and two feet tall; has a nose, two eyes, a mouth, ears, and hair. They lack eyelids and eyelashes. Their faces are golden brown and their bodies are emerald green.

The butterfly variety are delicate, dainty beings. They are no longer than an inch or two and generally live in greenhouses. Garden fairies are interested in human beings but for the most part, tolerate them. The fairies prefer babies who are more spontaneous and natural, like themselves.

Dora said the redwood forest fairies were especially interested in motor cars. They thought it strange to sit in a square box to move about, when their notion of motion is flying.

Water Fairies There are three main kinds of water fairies. Dora calls the fairies who live on the surface of the ocean, in sounds and bays—"water babies," because they look like round, fat, human babies. Water babies have great merry eyes in a whitish face; almost no hair, and faint knobs of ears. They have almost no feet and two, vague flipper-like hands. They roll and tumble against one another in the waves and have the jolliest of times.

They are the happiest of all the fairies and have a kindly feeling toward human beings whom they regard as solemn and serious.

Out on the high seas is a fairy of the middle deeps. This fairy is from five to seven feet tall and has a more distinctive human appearance. Their faces are elongated, with long noses and slit mouths. Their eyes are deep blue while their face is beige. They have sea-weedy hair, blue-black in color. Their body in enveloped in an indigo blue substance similar to floating chiffon. Their arms have no articulate endings and their legs are vague. Their quality is one of happiness but they are indifferent to human beings.

The third variety lives in the ocean depths. They are large like dark blue gorillas. They have little intelligence and only primitive emotions. They are made of a dense material which is almost visible to the physical eye. They seldom come to the surface and are hostile to human beings.

Fresh water fairies are quite different from sea fairies. There are tiny ones (eight inches to one foot) in small waterfalls and brooks; and a larger kind which ranges from two to three feet high. The smaller ones have perfect human faces and figures which are blue.

Fresh water fairies are more interested in human beings and they like to watch us. Like garden fairies and creatures of the woods, they love singing and can make beautiful music themselves.

Fire Fairies   There are two kinds. The small ones (three inches to two feet) have no human shape. They appear as foggy outlines. The tiny ones resemble candle flames and belong to the elemental class. They are not really fairies. Some look like insects, lizards, or beetles. They appear in little wood fires such as hearth fires and bonfires. They are called into being by the rhythm of the fire, which is the most powerful of vibrations. A harmonic invocation is created by the sound of the fire.

The larger ones (five feet to fourteen feet) are called

salamanders. The biggest salamanders live in volcanoes or may be present in forest fires.

Fire fairies have practically no relationship to humanity at all. Their only real connection is through their love of music. Most fairies are at least curious—but not so the salamander. Humans do not interest them.

Though fire in nature plays a destructive role, destruction is never random or casual as most people think. It is, instead, intelligently guided. Fire is both destructive, and at the same time a symbol of creation. Salamanders are the essence of fire, and are happy only where great displays of fire are to be seen.

Comment: I once had a reading done by a psychic at a fair. She told me each of us has an elf. (My elf is named Benjie.) Elves often talk in rhymes. She could see Benjie quite clearly. He was wearing a blue suede cowboy outfit, right down to suede western boots.

One time during a meditation, I sensed an elf for someone else in the circle. The elf seemed to be about one and one-half feet tall and was jolly. I could not see him . . . but I could sense him.

FAITH HEALING

Faith healing is accepting a healing on faith alone. You believe God can heal you, and the healing occurs.

One of the best known faith healers of our time was Kathryn Kuhlman. Her miracle services boasted of dramatic cures: a monstrous sixteen inch goiter vanishes instantly after thirty years; a terminally ill cancer patient is restored to health; a paralytic victim walks away from the services without crutches.

For years, Kathryn Kuhlman conducted services in the auditorium of the Carnegie Library in Pittsburgh, Pennsylvania. Thousands packed the auditorium seeking a healing of the physical body and deliverance from sin. Medical verification attests to the many physical healings which have occurred during these services. Kuhlman believed the healings occurred due to the Presence of the Holy Spirit. Because of the abundance of His Presence, sick bodies were healed— even the people waiting on the outside of the building for the doors to open. Kuhlman acted as the channel for the supernatural power of Almighty God. According to Kuhlman, faith is a gift. Faith begins where logic and reason end.

Allen Spragget, in his book *Kathryn Kuhlman: The Woman Who Believes in Miracles,* observed and analyzed Ms. Kuhlman's services. He watched as two ladies (who had been healed) were ushered to the stage, where Kathryn Kuhlman laid her hands on their heads. The ladies instantly collapsed. So common was this phenomenon, there were official catchers whose duty it was to prevent those who fell from injuring themselves.

Spraggett investigated other faith healers as well. Some experiences with faith healers have been negative; some have even spawned disastrous consequences. A teen-aged diabetic gave up her insulin and died. A boy who walked without crutches while on stage, had to resort to his crutches again in order to travel home. Is it any wonder that Oral Roberts' associates did not take kindly to a newspaper man poking around the "invalids' tent"? Spraggett discovered not one of the invalids showed the slightest improvement after the evangelist's brief visit. Spraggett's other investigations resulted in a long list of charlatans.

What then constitutes a miracle? Is one man's miracle another man's psychologically induced remission? Are we all susceptible to hysteria and gullibility?

Spraggett used the following criteria to describe a miraculous healing:

1. The disease should be a medically diagnosed organic or structural disorder.

2. The healing should be rapid, preferably quasi-instantaneous, and involve changes of a type not normally considered attributable to suggestion.

3. The healing should be permanent.

Spraggett found that genuine healings occurred at the Kuhlman services. He also found that miracles occur at Lourdes. (*See*
LOURDES.)

Comment: One night at a development class we took turns giving
spiritual healings to each other. When it was my turn to sit in the
chair, I suddenly felt a surge so powerful I thought I was going to pass
out. I asked to be allowed to lie down on the sofa. The lady who led
the group explained that I had opened myself in the third chakra
area. She explained that the energy was similar to water trying to get
through a pipe that was too small for the amount of pressure. The
feeling slowly subsided. Could this have been the power of the Holy
Spirit?—that same "Power" referred to by Kathryn Kuhlman?

FENG SHUI

Feng Shui (pronounced fung-shway), the Chinese art of place-
ment, is the result of over 3,000 years of observation of how people
are affected by the design, location, and arrangement of their homes
and workplaces. The best design and arrangement of a home or
workplace would promote and enhance harmony, health, balance,
and prosperity. Also taken into consideration is the flow of the Chi
(vital energy) through the space. When the environmental Chi is
improved, so is the Chi of its inhabitants.

FIRE WALKING

Fire walking is just that: it is the act of walking over a bed of
coals with surface temperatures up to five hundred degrees Celsius.
It used to be something that only the Indian fakirs and Hawaiian
Kahunas could do, but now there are fire-walking courses which you
can attend to learn how to do it for yourself. It is a case of mind over
matter . . . in a very real sense.

Comment: I don't think I'm ready to walk on a bed of hot coals just yet—but . . . if you think you can't, then you can't. What is it they say? State your limitations . . . and they are yours.

FLOWER ESSENCES

Flower essences are herbal preparations made from wild flowers and trees. They are sold in *stock bottles* from which a purchaser can make up individual *dosage bottles*. (Four drops under the tongue, four times per day is a standard dosage.)

Flower essences were first developed in their modern form in England in the 1930s by Dr. Edward Bach and have now been expanded to include many regional varieties with specific properties.

While no official claim can be made regarding healing effects, it is felt that these herbal infusions act as Nature's "liquid messengers" of inner health and harmony—especially affecting emotions, stress, mental attitudes, spiritual values, and life purpose. Bringing balance in the above areas is a major factor in creating mind-body health.

If food nourishes the human body, then *flower essences* nourish the human soul.

G

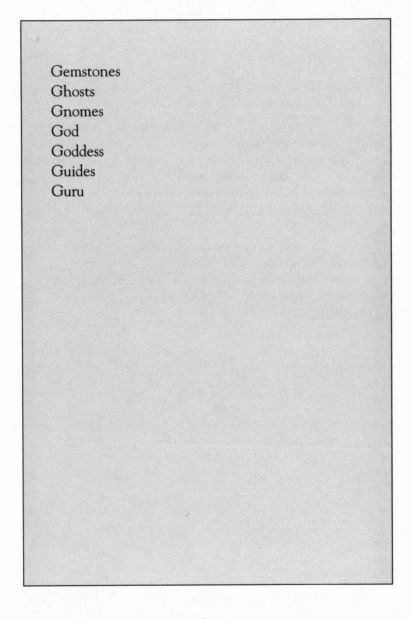

Gemstones
Ghosts
Gnomes
God
Goddess
Guides
Guru

GEMSTONES

Gemstones are thought to somehow focus the hidden energy of the universe and direct it toward spiritual awareness and healing. Gemstones can range from *agates* to *zircons*, and each is felt to possess a particular quality. Because *gemstones* possess a crystalline structure, they are able to collect, focus, and emit electromagnetic energy. We have already put crystals to work in a practical way: they transmit and receive radio waves, power our quartz watches, set the timing on our home computers, and release the sound energies from our favorite recordings. Even the effects of acupuncture are reported to increase by ten to twelve percent when the needles are coated with quartz crystal.

Gemstones can be worn, but are also effective placed about the household or work area, and function regardless of whether or not their properties are understood by the user.

When we are attracted to a particular gemstone, there is generally a need for that particular gemstone's vibration.

It would take too long to discuss each gemstone, but perhaps a list of stones associated with the zodiac signs is in order.

Aries—diamond	Libra—opal or tourmaline
Taurus—emerald	Scorpio—topaz
Gemini—moss agate or pearl	Sagittarius—lapis lazuli
Cancer—moonstone	Capricorn—ruby
Leo—onyx or smoky quartz	Aquarius—aquamarine
Virgo—sapphire	Pisces—amethyst

Comment: My birthstone and zodiac stone is diamond and emerald. "Diamonds are a girl's best friend." Too bad they are so expensive.

GHOSTS

Ghosts are usually the astral bodies of people who have died without the spiritual preparation they needed. Without foreknowledge of the spiritual realms, they cling closely to the physical world. (*See* EARTH-BOUND SPIRIT.)

Usually these entities are so upset or frightened that they are able to make some kind of impact on or around the place they "haunt." Sometimes they deliberately come to let you know they have survived death and that they are "alive and well."

Comment: When my grandmother was in her nineties, she and I made a pact.

"Grandma, if you can come and communicate with me after you pass over, will you?"

"I sure will, Elaine."

Two years later, my grandmother Franklin passed over the veil of death. A couple of months went by, with nothing unusual happening. Then one night, my (late) husband and I experienced what I believe to be a physical manifestation of Grandma's "ghost."

We were lying in bed, reading, at approximately nine in the evening. I suddenly heard some taps and thumps on the north side of the house. I commented that someone must have left the gate unfastened, and that it was blowing in the wind. The thumps and taps immediately moved to the south side of the house.

"Boy! The wind is really blowing," I said. "I can hear the lilac bushes hitting the house."

Both of us went back to our reading. Suddenly the noise shifted to the attic. It sounded as though a couple of squirrels were racing about inside. Drat! I thought to myself. How am I going to get those squirrels out of the attic? Just as quickly as the other shift, the thumps and bumps went under the house. Our cottage was on wooden posts at the time, and was completely open from the sides. My husband suggested that it sounded like dogs wagging their tails against the floor joists. We kept coming up with a physical explanation for the raps and thumps. Suddenly the entire house was surrounded by knocks and raps. One side. Other side. Attic. Under the house. Back and forth. There could no longer be a simple explanation.

"What the hell is that?" my husband asked.

"I know," I replied. "I'll bet it's Grandma!"

The moment I recognized the source, a most amazing thing happened. A loud rapport outside my bedroom window occurred, with the same volume of noise as if someone had exploded a shotgun shell. Both of us jumped at the sudden noise. The window was not open, yet the drapes flew out about a foot, then went back in again. The noise has never occurred since—but I have had two mediums make reference to a window during their readings for me. One lady was a trance-medium from Scotland who was doing a past-life reading when she was interrupted by a lady from the side of the "mama parent," who kept talking about a window.

I feel this is confirmation of the night Grandma came to let me know she is "alive and well," and kept her promise to communicate between the spiritual and physical realms.

GNOMES

Gnomes are Earth Fairies which live close to, or under rocks. They are short, dumpy, and gray-brown in color. Their limbs are one color, and their bodies are another. Usually the body is darker than the legs and arms. Their feet are large, pointed, and not very shapely which gives them the effect of wearing pointed shoes. Their arms are long and their hands are lumpy (not very well defined). The space between the nose and eyes on their face is wider than in human beings. This gives the head a flattened, shovel-like appearance. The chin is long and sharp suggesting a beard, while their heads have the appearance of being covered with a conventional cap.

Gnomes do not like human beings. They emerge from under rocks to peer at human intruders. Generally they exist in groups of four or five. They have definite likes and dislikes, but their intelligence is not very high, and their emotions are rather primitive. They regard rocks as their friends and living beings.

Comment: I met a lady who claims she used to see trolls when she was a little girl. She claimed each bridge has a troll living under its structure. Gives a whole new slant to the story of "The Three Billy Goats Gruff," doesn't it?

GOD

Throughout history mankind has had many names for God. Some of them are: Allah, Yahweh, 'Elohim, I Am, Jehovah, Emmanuel, The Force, The Supreme Intelligence, The Cosmic Mind, Infinite One, The Divine Mind, The Universal Mind, Divine Love, The Divine Spirit, and Mother/Father/God.

Of course there are many more words for God—but I think you get the point. Does it really matter what name we choose for God? I don't think so. What *is* important for us to realize is the concept that a spark of God is in each and every one of us. Because that Divine Spark is part of us, the best way to find God is to go within.

GODDESS

A *goddess* is a female god. Therefore, a goddess has all the attributes of a god: immortality, supernatural power, and the ability to create universes and rule over them.

In Egyptian myth, the goddess *Isis* was very powerful. She was normally represented as a woman bearing on her head a throne (later, a disc between cow's horns). She was openly worshipped into Christian times. She parallels the Christian version of the immaculate conception by giving birth to Horus.

In St. Germain-des-Prés, a church built (A.D. 542) over a former temple of Isis, there is a black statue of Isis—worshipped as the Virgin Mary until 1514.

The image of the High Priestess (Tarot card, A. E. Waite version) is that of Isis.

In England (1920s) the Fraternity of the Inner Light was founded to reestablish *Isis* as an image of dynamic womanhood, active rather than passive, and capable of operating as an awakening, transformative power.

Isis represents the archetypal virginity of the feminine side of God. She is more than a pagan Egyptian goddess; she is a great force of transformation, change, and growth.

Today, we are recognizing a new goddess . . . GAIA, the Earth-goddess (Earth-Mother).

Comment: As you know, I was raised with the traditional patriarchal values of Christianity. When I first attended a Spiritualist church (as an adult), I remember the Reverend (a female) opening the service with prayer. Her first words were: "Divine Spirit, Mother/Father/God." Up until that point, I had never considered the female aspect of God. I adopted those words for myself, and over the years my perspective and philosophy of life has changed.

GUIDES

Guides are spiritual teachers or masters who assist us while we are on the physical plane. They can range from recently departed souls to entities which have never experienced an earthly incarnation. Some guides claim to be visitors from distant galaxies. Usually, they come with overwhelming love and unconditional service. Their wisdom and knowledge teaches and comforts us . . . and we begin to know a peace within, we never knew before.

Comment: Shortly after we arrived in B.C., Wesley and I began a long stint of daily meditations. A "being" came to me one day during an inward journey, and I have since referred to this entity as my guide. I shall duplicate three pages from my journal, so you can see how I met "Tulma."

Morning Meditation: June 17, 1989

Sent purple, green, and gold to the thieves who robbed us as Faye instructed us to do. I saw a pudding mold. I was told that spirit was molding me, preparing me. I told them that was all fine and dandy, but I wanted to be consciously aware, instead of "going out" all the time. They said not to worry about it; that practice and discipline would fix the short circuit. They compared the work they are doing with me to a video-recorder. Everything has been recorded, but until the short-circuit for channel three has been cleared up, it won't play back.

I told them it was good to get some verbal communication again, and asked them what their names were.

"Don't worry about names. There are many of us. Call us 'Beings of Light' . . . but since you asked . . . I am Tulma. And this is Sinab. All of our names harmonize with the vibration of 'Beings of Light'."

Then I "went out." The sound of ravens at the bird feeder brought me back.

Morning Meditation: June 29, 1989

"I am Tulma, leader of the Annasini tribe. My name is revered by my subjects. We are the 'Beings of Light'."

Mental questions and answers:

Q. What are you here to do?
A. We are leading you along your spiritual path.
Q. What am I to do?
A. Learn to open your spiritual eye and close your physical eye.
Q. How do I do that?
A. By doing what you are doing. Meditate regularly and keep practicing. When you learned to play the piano, you suddenly realized one day, that you had arrived. You could play. It was a gradual thing, but you knew you had arrived. It is the same with spiritual development. One day, you will have just "arrived."

Morning Meditation: July 5, 1989

The three lessons of light:

ook
earn
ove

Q. What am I supposed to do? What is my work that I am to do?

I saw a hand pick up an old-fashioned plume pen, dip it into the ink, and write in fancy script, a single word:

Write!

"Go now, and walk in the light."

Later in July, a friend of mine and her husband flew to B.C. to spend a week with us. Since my friend had been a reverend in the spiritualist church in Ontario for a number of years or so, they joined Wesley and myself in our morning meditations.

My friend, clearly saw our "beings of light," and drew one of them for us. It was a nebulous figure of shimmering light mixed with soft shades of violet. This confirmed for me that my Tulma is very real indeed.

GURU

In Hinduism, a *guru* is one's personal teacher and spiritual adviser; but any leader who is highly regarded by a group of followers is considered to be a "guru."

During the 1970s, Maharishi Mahesh Yogi toured the United States. He was considered to be a wise guru; and was responsible, along with others, for launching TM, known as Transcendental Meditation. This technique of meditating was introduced to literally millions of people. (*See* TRANSCENDENTAL.)

H

Halos
Healings
Higher Self
Horoscope
Host
Huna

HALOS

Halos are rings or patches of light which surround the heads of angels, saints, and Christ. At least that is what the old master painters would lead us to believe. Who has not seen a picture of the Christ, without noticing the yellow light painted around the head?

Halos are a part of the human aura which I believe most people could see with the naked eye, many years ago. Somehow, we have almost lost this gift. (*For further information, see* AURAS.)

HEALINGS

Healings are physical changes brought about in the human body by a variety of methods. When our body is in a state of "dis-ease," we need to look for a method that will put the body back in balance again. Healings can be effected by: faith healing (*see* FAITH HEALING), bathing in the waters at Lourdes (*see* LOURDES), waiting for Mother Nature, visualizing wellness, going to a doctor, taking medications, not taking medications, reflexology, iridology, working with crystals, working with sounds, working with colors, polarity balancing, a massage, visiting a psychiatrist, visiting a shaman, visiting a holistic practitioner, acupuncture, aroma-therapy, chiropractic treatments, colonic irrigations, kinesiology, meditation, using Chi Gong, using Reiki, and using prayer . . . to name a few. The point is: Ultimately, we are each responsible for our own health or "dis-ease."

HIGHER SELF

Many philosophies teach that man is made up of three parts: the physical, or conscious; the sub-conscious; and the higher self, or superconscious. Our higher self is the spiritual portion of our identities. It is that portion of ourselves which is connected to the Universal Mind, or God, if you like. We can get in touch with ourselves by getting in touch with the higher self. Our "higher self " is very wise and can tell us all we need to know. Look within. Ask . . . and it will be answered unto you.

HOROSCOPE

A *horoscope* is an astrological illustration of the position of the sun, moon, and planets from a given latitude and longitude on earth at a given moment, usually that of birth. The construction of the horoscope is based on the Ptolemaic system in which the earth is stationary and the heavenly bodies move around it in fixed patterns.

Astrologers have divided the heavens into twelve sections, each thought to be ruled by a different sign of the zodiac belt through which the sun, moon, and planets move—in twelve fixed positions called houses. Once the particular sign and houses have been established, the mythological characteristics of the heavenly bodies, modified by the geometrical relationship between them, are used to foretell events in the life of the individual for whom the horoscope has been drawn. The twelve houses, and the corresponding dates are listed below, if you want to locate your birth date in order to learn more about your individual horoscope.

♈	*Aries:*	The Ram	March 21 - April 19
♉	*Taurus:*	The Bull	April 20 - May 20
♊	*Gemini:*	The Twins	May 21 - June 20
♋	*Cancer:*	The Crab	June 21 - July 22
♌	*Leo:*	The Lion	July 23 - August 22
♍	*Virgo:*	The Maiden	August 23 - September 22
♎	*Libra:*	The Scales	September 23 -October 22
♏	*Scorpio:*	The Scorpion	October 23 - November 21
♐	*Sagittarius:*	The Archer	November 22 - December 21
♑	*Capricorn:*	The Goat	December 22 - January 19

♒ *Aquarius:*   The Water Carrier January 20 - February 18
♓ *Pisces:*   The Fishes   February 19 - March 20

(Also *see* ASTROLOGY; ZODIAC.)

Symbols of the Planets, Sun, and Moon

☽ Moon   ☉ Sun
☿ Mercury   ♀ Venus
♂ Mars   ♃ Jupiter
♄ Saturn   ♅ Uranus
♆ Neptune   ♇ Pluto

HOST

A *host* is a small wafer used in the Catholic Church (and others) for communion services. The consecrated host represents the body of Christ in memory of the Last Supper in which Jesus infused his Spirit into the bread.

HUNA

The word *Huna* is an ancient Hawaiian word which originally meant "secret." It refers to the Ancient Wisdom which once was passed on only to specially chosen students of the great masters of ancient times. This important knowledge is therefore not exclusively "Hawaiian" in nature, but belongs to all peoples and all languages. However, much of the recovered "secret" knowledge was coded into the language of ancient Hawaii, and *Huna* is still a good name to identify that system of psychology which seeks after knowledge of the complete make-up of a person. (*See* KAHUNA.)

I

I Ching
Illumination
Incense
Indigenous People
Intuition

I CHING

The *I Ching*, pronounced ee ching, or "Book of Changes" is an ancient Chinese text of philosophical thought used for divination. The version that has come down to our time was edited and annotated by Confucius. Modern people still consult this oracle of sixty-four hexagrams for insight and guidance. The oracle is consulted by counting forty-nine yarrow sticks in a given way or casting three coins. The *I Ching* is primarily a book of wisdom whose underlying idea is that everything changes. One who perceives the meaning of change no longer fixes his attention on transitory individual things, but on the eternal law of change at work in all life. In addition, the visible world is seen as symbolic of our inner world, and the ultimate goal is to live, in this world of opposites, beyond duality in harmony with all nature.

ILLUMINATION

Illumination refers to the "enlightenment" of the mind. Illumination is a kind of intuitive knowledge imparted to the individual directly, from transcendental sources.

INCENSE

Incense consists of sweet or spicy scented sticks which burn very slowly, to give off a sweet-smelling smoke. This sensual aid is believed to help in the heightening of the consciousness, during prayer or meditation. Some feel that the scent of incense, especially that of sandalwood, attracts the blessing and help of teachers in the spiritual realms.

INDIGENOUS PEOPLE

Indigenous people is another way of saying *native people*. These are the inhabitants who belonged to the land as the original people.

In the U.S.A. and Canada, we have the *North American Indian*. There is also the *Inuit* (Eskimo) and the *Aleut*.

The *Mayas* (Yucatan, Belize, and N. Guatemala) had a highly developed civilization when discovered by Europeans in the sixteenth century.

The *Incas* dominated ancient Peru until the Spanish conquest.

There are the *Pygmies* of Africa and Asia, and the *Aborigines* of Australia.

All of the indigenous people have a common thread running through their history. Their culture, their health, their dignity, their very way of life . . . has been disrupted by the invasion of the white man. The white man has conquered, pillaged, and spread his diseases to many of the indigenous people. The white man has a lot to answer for. Maybe it is time to learn some of the "ancient wisdom" from the native peoples—before the knowledge is lost forever.

The indigenous people, in general, know how to live and work in harmony with nature. These "primitive" people have much to teach (so-called) "*civilized*" man.

INTUITION

Intuitive knowledge is that knowledge which flashes suddenly into our consciousness from seemingly out of nowhere. It is what most people call a hunch or "gut feeling." We just *know*. Our intuition can serve as a useful tool, but only if we pay attention to it. (*See* E.S.P.)

J

Jesus, the Christ
Jung, Carl

JESUS, THE CHRIST

Jesus, the Christ was the God-man of the ages. He lived to show the possibilities of man. Following is a quote from the Aquarian Gospel 68: 11-14:

> Men call me Christ, and God has recognized the name; but Christ is not a man. The Christ is universal love, and Love is king.
> This Jesus is but man who has been fitted by temptations overcome, by trials multiform, to be the temple through which Christ can manifest to men.
> Then hear, you men of Israel, hear! Look not upon the flesh; it is not king. Look to the Christ within, who shall be formed in every one of you, as he is formed in me.
> When you have purified your hearts by faith, the king will enter in, and you will see his face.

Comment: Look to the Christ within. (*Also* see ESSENES.)

JUNG, CARL (1875-1961)

Carl Jung was a great Swiss psychoanalyst and seer. He analyzed over sixty-seven thousand dreams before beginning to theorize about their meaning and function. He evolved "word association" tests to make hidden material conscious. He saw psychosis as arising from the arrested development of an individual's personal maturity. He supported Freud, despite his doubts about Freud's concept of sex as the main subconscious driving force. Jung and Freud were friends until a disagreement over a dream and a "catalytic exteriorization phenomenon" (loud report, i.e. noise from the bookcase) forced them to part company.

Jung developed theories of the collective unconscious. His book *The Psychology of Type* empirically examined consciousness. He divided the Self into four functions: thinking/feeling (rational), and intuition/sensation (non-rational). He believed health requires the balance of the four functions by making repressed material conscious. (*See* SUBCONSCIOUS.)

In 1944 Jung had a near-death experience whereby his spirit left his body, and he looked down at the earth from a great height. He saw the form of his doctor rise up from the direction of Europe, with a message sent by the earth. There was a protest against Jung's "going away." Jung returned to his body for another seventeen years.

Today, Jung's thinking and pioneer work, like that of Freud's, permeates Western psychological approaches to therapy.

K

Kabala
Kahuna
Karma
Kashic Records
Kundalini

KABALA or KABBALA or QABBALAH

The word *Kabala* is from the ancient Hebrew, and means: "doctrines received by ancient traditions." The oral teachings traditionally are said to date back to the time of the Secret Wisdom related to Moses.

The basic teaching of the Kabala is that the universe is unity which works according to a set pattern. The universe is God, and man is part of God, so consequently man is also part of the universe. Therefore, if man can grow until he becomes God, he controls the universe.

The key to growth is knowledge. This knowledge is attained by divine revelations. The revelations are achieved by understanding God. To know God is to become one with Him. To understand God, you must first understand yourself. This can be done by studying the planets and numbers which are regarded as stepping stones that lead back up the ten paths of God (the Sephiroth) to unity with the Creator. The knowledge which is needed to achieve unity with God is also believed to be contained in the Bible. Kabalists believe the Bible contains the actual word of God; by studying the Bible, divine knowledge can be acquired. However, so only the chosen will learn its secrets, it is written in code and each word must be decoded separately if the real meaning is to be found.

The most important Kabalistic works are: *The Book of Formation* and *The Zohar*. Both deal with the exile of man from God, his descent through the ten spheres that comprise the universe, and the ways he can work his way back again. Kabalistic writings are couched in a language of contradiction so that only those who have achieved the divine knowledge can fully understand them.

This Jewish book of wisdom (the *Kabala*) attempts to explain how the apparent chaos of the universe fits its multitude of opposites into an intelligible pattern; and how man's relationship with God and the world fit with the entire cosmological plan.

KAHUNA

The *Kahuna* is the Hawaiian counterpart to a *shaman* or *medicine man*.

Max Freedom Long spent eighteen years researching the secrets of the Hawaiian kahunas and his book *Rediscovering the Ancient Magic* was subsequently published. His book led to the founding of the Huna Research Associates.

Long attempted to penetrate beyond the externals of native magic and discover its basic secret. He felt the old Magic, once the heritage of humanity, was lost in Christendom for centuries. Only recently are we beginning to recover it.

Long was especially fascinated with the kahunas' ability to walk on beds of hot coals in their bare feet without burning their flesh. He was impressed with the kahunas' ability to heal. Long cites many cases which include materialization, levitation, brownies, poltergeists, trances, the invocation of angels, and even the manipulation of the growth of a man's whiskers.

From the Huna Research comes material which teaches prayer-actions. Man is made up of three parts: the High Self (Superconscious), the Middle Self (Conscious), and the Lower Self (Sub-conscious).

Mana equals *Vital Force* (symbol: water). It can be increased by asking it to be, and visualizing the *mana* rising like a fountain.

The Huna teachings state: the Low Self must contact the High Self by activating the *aka* thread and sending some of the surcharge of *mana* to the High Self. At the same time, we request that the High Self use our thought forms to create the desired prayer requests.

Of course, we should never ask for something which might hurt another.

Practice + patience = results. (*See* HUNA.)

KARMA

The law of *Karma* is inseparable from the process of re-incarnation by which the spirit returns to earth in a series of lives. Each life is necessary to work out debts owing from previous ones and the circle is only broken if and when the spirit is set free by shedding all conflicting emotions. In this way, it becomes detached from the material world and therefore does not suffer from the consequences of its actions. Once this has been achieved, the spirit has no further need of physical incarnations and begins its progress to higher planes of existence.

The theory of karma is used as an explanation for why all men are not born equal, and why some always seem to be luckier than others. Karma would seem to entail complete predestination, but this is not the case. The individual is responsible for his own karma and if he did not have free will, he would not be able to go wrong or right, and so, could not benefit from his actions.

Karmic penalties are not flexible but can be alleviated by a change of attitude on the part of the individual. This is particularly the case with physical karma when a person is afflicted with disease in one life to match the results of his actions in another. Depending on the seriousness of his previous actions, he can lessen his suffering by a complete break from the character traits he may still be harboring from previous incarnations. He then becomes a better person in all senses of the word. The law of karma does not only apply from life to life, but also from day to day. Sometimes a good or bad action or thought brings an almost immediate result. For example, you help another person and soon after, need similar help yourself, which you receive from a totally unexpected source. Most people would call this luck; others would see it as the logical effect of the karmic laws.

Karma, then, is a term used to mean the working of the law of compensation. For each sorrow or pain we cause another, we shall suffer in like degree and manner, and at a time when the lesson to be gained thereby will be most impressive. The sole purpose of compensation is to teach us a lesson, to make us realize the error, and advance our understanding. The law of balances works both ways: a human being may have a karmic debt due *to* him. He will thus be in line as a recipient of compensation.

Karmic law states: For every action, there must be an equal and positive reaction. In other words . . . what you sow is what you reap. Sometimes this law operates very quickly. You may reap this afternoon, what you have sown this morning. Or, it may take another lifetime, to reap what you have sown in past lives.

KASHIC RECORDS

(See AKASHIC RECORDS.*)*

KUNDALINI

Sexual orgasm is important for the physical well-being of a person. The orgasm bathes the body in life energy. When done with love and respect for your mate, sexual intercourse is a holy experience, satisfying the deep primordial urges of mating on the physical level, and the deep spiritual yearnings of uniting with Divinity. It is a marriage of the spiritual and physical aspects of two human beings.

Kundalini yoga is a spiritual discipline which states that a physical discharge is no longer necessary for the well-being of a person. The spiritual practice of using meditation to contain, transform, and redirect the sexual energy along different energy channels is known as *Kundalini*. By moving the sexual energy along the vertical power current up the spine, it is transformed into higher vibratory energy which is then used to build the higher spiritual bodies. This is a very powerful and potentially dangerous practice, and must be done with guidance.

Kundalini is sometimes called "the sleeping princess," but its literal meaning is: "a bowl of fire." Sometimes, kundalini is represented as the serpent which rises from the bowl—it is the fiery serpent. In its higher aspect, *serpent* means wisdom; but its lower aspect is that of tempter.

So, kundalini, located at the root chakra, is the center where great creative power lies. It is the center of the sex power. Used rightly, it can be the greatest, most holy, and mighty power for good. It can also be very dangerous if this energy rises up the incorrect channels, or too suddenly.

L

Lemuria
Lessons
Levitation
Life Force
Light Grids
Lineage
Lourdes
Lucid Dreaming

LEMURIA

The lost continent of Lemuria (known as Mu) is believed to have existed off the western coast of California and stretched to the shores of Asia.

There were two factions of the civilization of Lemuria. One civilization walked in a Love expression. They were interested primarily in growth, expanding their knowledge, and doing the Father's work. Their main focus was to establish proper energy vortexes, or patterns, to prepare the planet for compatibility with evolved future beings.

The other faction was one of warring beings. They were more interested in power. Their minds were highly developed, but they used their abilities in a most destructive manner.

In between, there was a strain of mutants who were the labor force for both factions. These beings were of comparatively low intelligence, but quite large and physically strong to enable them to perform manual labor—which was primarily their function and their purpose.

Lemuria and its civilizations were in existence for slightly over 100,000 years. Around 85,000 B.C., the earth's crust shifted and Lemuria sank beneath the ocean. (*See* ATLANTIS.)

The only remains of Mu, are: the Easter Islands and part of Hawaii.

LESSONS

Our spirit enters the physical plane so it can gain experience, acquire knowledge, and grow spiritually. These experiences are sometimes referred to as *lessons*. Apparently we can progress at a much faster rate on the earth plane than we can in the spiritual realms. That is why souls are eager to come to earth . . . to learn. We return many times polishing different facets of our totality. If we think of our soul as an uncut jewel, perhaps it is easier to understand.

Through various experiences undergone by the soul on earth, that jewel is being slowly, but surely, cut and polished. Each facet of the jewel represents an earthly lifetime where the soul has been developing and perfecting one special aspect of itself. A soul can appear more spiritual in one lifetime and not so spiritual in the next. One lifetime might perfect the emotional body; another lifetime, the mental body. As each facet is cut and polished, we pass through various stages of unfoldment. The soul learns balance and beauty, as it aspires towards God.

Comment: I swear my lesson in this lifetime is to learn "patience." (But please God, I want it right now.)

LEVITATION

Levitation is a process which reverses the polarities of a substance, relating to gravity. If a material is no longer subject to gravity—think of the possibilities. If the gigantic stones of the pyramids were not subject to gravity, they could be manipulated into place easily. We have all seen the lady levitated into the air during the circus act, but is levitation fact or fiction?

A renowned Chinese doctor from Canton reports that one day, as a seventeen-year-old student, he visited his 107-year-old teacher. Slipping into the meditation room as quietly as possible, he paused to look through the chinks in the wall and saw his teacher, seated in the lotus position, hovering in the air midway between the ceiling and his meditation cushion. That was enough to convince the young man that these powers come from a profound knowledge of the human energy system and its perfect balance.

Comment: I'm not sure you would call the following experience true levitation, but it certainly surprised a few of the students at our Human Awareness class. The instructor asked for a "heavy" volunteer to sit on a chair at the front of the room. The person who volunteered, weighed well over two hundred pounds. Next, four people were asked to assist in the levitation (in this case, lifting) act. Each of the four assistants were told to clasp their hands together and extend only their index fingers. Two people stood on one side of the subject, with two on the opposite side. Two assistants each placed their extended index fingers (hands clasped) under the armpits of the subject. The other two, placed their fingers under the knees of the subject. When asked to *lift*, they made a feeble attempt to lift the subject off the chair. The subject may have left the chair temporarily by a quarter of an inch, but basically, the attempt was futile.

Then the four assistants were asked to count to seven simultaneously, while stacking their out-stretched palms on the top of the subject's head. (The reason for a "seven" count—is because one palm was stationed there before the countdown.) One person placed one palm on top of the palm already in place . . . then alternated with the other three until all palms were stacked on the subject's head. All counted, "One , two, three, four, five, six, seven." At the end of "seven," hands clasped for the second time—index fingers pointing out—two under the armpits, two under the knees, they tried the lift again. Amazingly enough, they were able to lift the subject three to four feet straight into the air, with the ease of lifting a pillow. The eyes of the "heavy" subject were a surprise to behold. I have participated in such antics. How does it work? I don't know . . . but *it works*.

LIFE FORCE

Without the *life force* flowing through us, our physical body would be dead. There have been many names given to the life force throughout history. The Hawaiians called it *Mana;* the Chinese— *Ch'i;* the Egyptians—*Ka;* the Japanese—*Reiki;* and the people of India—*Prana.* Today some metaphysicians refer to it as *vital energy* or *bio-cosmic energy.*

The root chakra is the location of the first manifestation of the life force in the physical world. When the life force is fully functioning through this center, the person has a powerful will to live in the physical reality. When the life force is fully functioning through the three lowest chakras, combined with a powerful flow down the legs, the individual makes a clear and direct statement of physical potency. Power and vitality emanate from him, in the form of vital energy. Often he acts as a generator by energizing those around him, recharging their energy systems.

Comment: Have you ever met someone who literally "charges your batteries?" They seem to exude so much energy; you feel better just by being in their presence.

LIGHT GRIDS

As cells are essential structures to our physical body, light grids are "invisible" energy structures for new "light bodies." When activated, these grids transfer higher dimensional energies into our bodies, helping us to embody more expansive states of consciousness.

LINEAGE

A line of succession of teachers who continue throughout time to transmit spiritual teachings in unbroken purity.

LOURDES

Lourdes is a famous Roman Catholic shrine. It is located in a town of about ten thousand inhabitants in the foothills of the Pyrenees in southern France. It is estimated two million pilgrims a year flock to Lourdes. Some are so desperately ill that helpers are needed. The ill bathe in the icy water which flows from an underground spring, hoping for a miracle—and indeed they do occur.

Over one hundred years ago, a French peasant girl saw visions of the one she called "The Lady." Since that time, there have been thousands of claimed healings at Lourdes. Some of these healings have been officially proclaimed by the Roman Catholic Church as canonical miracles. The Medical Bureau at Lourdes displays x-rays to prove some of the dramatic healings. No cure is accepted until it has stood the test of time (normally three years). Any doctor is free to visit the Medical Bureau to examine records. They may also take part in interviewing a person who claims a cure. Hundreds of doctors are registered at the Bureau. They include: Catholics, Protestants, Jews, Muslims, Hindus, and assorted free thinkers. Are the healings at Lourdes beyond medical explanation? The answer appears to be yes.

Lourdes is a special place. "The Lady" appeared eighteen times to Bernadette Soubirous, a fourteen-year-old farmer's daughter, while she was praying in the grotto at Lourdes. "The Lady" gave instructions that a church was to be built on the spot, and today a huge sanctuary stands atop the grotto. The apparition also told Bernadette to dig in the ground inside the grotto. A spring instantly gushed forth. It has been flowing ever since at the rate of 27,000 gallons of water a day. Millions have bathed in it. This shrine of Lourdes is, indeed, a place of miracles, as are many other places where Mother Mary has been reported to appear, such as Fatima in Portugal, Beauraing and Banneux in Belgium, The Weeping Madonna of Syracuse in Sicily, and more recently (1981), Medugorje in Yugoslavia where the "Madonna"—The Mother of God—appeared repeatedly to six children on Mount Crnica.

LUCID DREAMING

Lucid dreaming is the act of dreaming while the dreamer is fully aware he or she is dreaming. It is believed that by learning to control your dreams, you can increase your psychic powers and creativity.

Dreams occur during periods of sleep where there is rapid eye movement (REM).

You can become your own expert dream interpreter. Keep a regular dream diary. The more you practice, the more you will remember. Note your feelings when you awaken. Your mood is an important key to the meaning of your dream. By establishing a firm connection between your waking mind and your dreams, you are ready to try problem-solving while you sleep.

Comment: I have reached the point where I can tell myself I am having a bad dream, and therefore I will wake myself up to escape it. Nine times out of ten, I do wake up. Also, I have learned to say to myself (while I am dreaming), "this is really interesting—I must remember this when I wake up." Most of the time I do remember the desired passage. It only backfired on me once:

I was experiencing a frustrating dream where I could not find my car, and I had lost my purse. Since everything was so confused, I decided that I must be dreaming, so I woke myself up. When I went to my sister's house to ask for help, she explained that she had helped me search for the car half the night. Didn't I remember? I could not remember the search; I could not find my purse. I felt even more confused and heartsick. Then I woke up . . . this time for real. (*See* DREAMS.)

M

Mana
Mandala
Manifesting
Mantra
Master
Materialization
Medicine Man/Woman
Meditation
Medium
Metaphysics
Mind

MANA

Mana is the Hawaiian word for "life force" or "vital force." Its symbol is water. It is believed that we can increase our mana by breathing deeply and visualizing mana rising in us like a fountain. Men are to breathe from above while women are to breathe from below. By sending a surcharge of mana to the higher self with instructions to the lower self to contact the higher self, it is believed that visualized or desired conditions can be built into the future so that they will appear as realities in the present. These thought forms are always sent on a flow of mana.

MANDALA

In Hinduism and Buddhism, a *mandala* is a graphic symbol of the universe. It is a circular design, containing concentric geometric forms, images of deities etc., and symbolizes the universe, totality, and wholeness.

Comment: When Tibetan lamas visited the Hopi elders in Arizona in the early 1980s, each group laid out complicated sand-painting mandalas. Both were amazed to see how similar were the colors, patterns, and meanings.

MANIFESTING

The new age philosophy suggests that each of us creates his/her own reality. A lot of what we are experiencing was decided by *us*, long before we entered the physical body for our sojourn on the earth plane. However, there still remains free choice. We can make choices along the way. If we are not happy with the way our lives are going, we can change by changing our attitudes. We can use positive affirmations to begin the upward spiral. We can use visualizations and any number of other tools, to manifest the desirable conditions in our lives. It all begins with the realization that: "You are responsible for you," and no one else.

Comment: Wesley and I had been sitting on a warm rock in the middle of the Similkameen River in B.C. While basking in the sun, we took turns reading aloud from a book about Findhorn. We discussed the possibilities of manifesting desired things in our lives.

Wesley went for a philosophical walk. I remained on the rock. For several weeks prior to this occasion, we had visited numerous car dealerships. We wanted to trade our converted '88 van for an '88 truck with an extended cab. We had calculated values, and decided our van was worth more than a new truck. We had just purchased a house and could use the $3500 difference to purchase appliances come closing date. We received many offers, but no one wanted to trade our van for a new truck and give us $3500 besides. One dealership offered to trade even, but that is the closest we came out of half a dozen proposals.

I had made up my mind we were not going to give the van away—even if we had to keep it. As I sat on that rock, I thought about the van, the truck, life in general, and manifesting. Suddenly, I spoke aloud: "If there is anything at all to this manifesting stuff—manifest a new truck in exchange for this van, and give me at least $3500 as well . . . so I can buy my appliances." I said it with intense emotion and clarity of purpose. Just then Wesley returned. We jumped into the van and drove back to the motel.

The next morning we awoke, had breakfast, then Wesley asked: "What do you want to do today?" I instantly thought of Kelowna. I was not familiar with Kelowna, but I knew it was a fairly big place. (Wesley had gone to school there when he was a boy.)

"I want to go to Kelowna and look for a truck," I stated.

Wesley was agreeable. The trip would take us at least two hours. By the time we reached Summerland, it was raining. It had turned into an ugly day, so we stopped for lunch along the lake.

"Do you still want to go to Kelowna, or shall we turn back?" Wesley questioned. He felt that the car dealership would not be any different from the rest.

"Yes. I want to go to Kelowna." The impression was quite compelling.

To make a long story short . . . we went to the car dealership and traded our van for a new truck. We also received $3900 difference, enough to pay for running boards on the truck and buy the appliances for the house. This was a clear indication to me that manifesting does indeed work.

Perhaps we really do create our own reality after all.

MANTRA

A *mantra* is a word or phrase, chanted, sung, hummed, or heard within the mind. It is used to create the calmness and vibratory level necessary for effective meditation.

Some people have their own personal mantra. Others use the word OM. The mantra helps to remove all other thoughts and interference from the mind.

The word *mantra* is derived from Sanskrit, and means: "the sound whose effects are known."

MASTER

A *master* is someone who has attained some degree of perfection in the evolution of the soul. While we have visible and invisible masters who teach us, the ultimate goal is for each of us to become our own master. Through meditation, we can receive messages from the invisible Masters.

Jesus, the Christ, was often referred to as "Master."

MATERIALIZATION

A *materialization* occurs when ectoplasm (*see* ECTOPLASM) is used to produce a semi-solid form which is capable of talking in a manner similar to when the spirit was on the earth plane. The trance medium sets up a cabinet in the corner of a room. A cabinet consists of black curtains which are hung. Usually there is a red light which enables the sitters to see the shapes as they form out of the ectoplasm from the medium. Unless invited to do so, the sitters should not touch the forms, as it could do damage to the medium. Materialization mediumship is rare today, but was quite popular some years ago in the Spiritualist Church.

Comment: I had the privilege of interviewing the late Reverend Gertrude Lievers in Brantford Ontario, when she was eighty-six years of age. She was one of the founders of the Hope Memorial Spiritualist Church and had witnessed several spirit materializations. One of Reverend Liever's daughters had died at the young age of thirty-three during childbirth. During a sitting, this daughter stepped out from the medium's cabinet and said, "Hi ya Mom." The daughter put her arms around Reverend Lievers and gave her a kiss. Reverend Lievers claimed her daughter felt just as solid as you or I.

Reverend Lievers also saw a lady walked around the room by her three departed husbands. All twenty of the sitters saw them. Three men materialized—all from the medium's body.

Reverend Lievers saw a young boy materialize and walk on his mother's arm while singing "I Love You Truly."

These materializations occurred at some of the spiritualist camps located in the U.S.A. Reverend Lievers did not know of any materialization mediums living in Canada.

Plaster casts of spirit materializations have been taken using melted paraffin wax. A mold was secured of a child's hand and a child's foot. The creases in the skin, and veins were visible. These could only have been produced by a materialization followed by a dematerialization—the latter being necessary to disengage the hand from the paraffin "glove." Those who have taken such casts, claim small pieces of skin are left behind when a form dematerializes. They claim to have verified this, by looking at the skin under a microscope.

MEDICINE MAN/WOMAN

(*See* SHAMAN).

MEDITATION

Meditation is an inward journey into the realms of consciousness known as an "altered state of consciousness." Our brain waves slow down to an alpha or theta state (*see* BRAIN WAVE FREQUENCIES) measurable by an electroencephalograph. The whole concept of meditation is directed towards developing the use of more of the mind. To this end, we must discover and operate the subjective or inner aspects of our minds. The deeper dimensions of our minds contain all the tools and equipment we need to function at the inner levels of awareness.

By going within, we come in contact with that spark of the Divine, our higher selves. If we learn to listen to our higher selves and all the higher guides and teachers, we shall live an abundant, harmonious life.

Comment: There are many methods of meditation which can lead to channeling, mediumship, or simply a greater spiritual awareness. Here is the method I use:

Find a comfortable position, either sitting or lying down. Close your eyes. Take three or four deep breaths, inhaling through the nose and exhaling through the mouth. Concentrate on your body and mentally tell each part of your body to relax, from the toes on your feet to the muscles in your face. Tense some of your muscles, then let them relax. While in this relaxed state, visualize the color red. You can imagine yourself inhaling and exhaling the color red. Move to the color orange; and while you are visualizing this color, allow your emotions to relax. Move to the color yellow . . . and allow your mental activity to cease. Hold only the color yellow in your mind. Move to the color green. Allow peace and healing to surround you, and penetrate you. Move to the color blue. Feel the Love of God encompass you. Move to the color indigo. Concentrate on your dreams and aspirations. Feel yourself going deeper and deeper within. Finally, concentrate on the color violet. Tell yourself you are now in touch with your spiritual self. From here, you can journey to a place in nature such as a beach or a mountain, where you can be alone, where you can feel at peace. Sometimes when you have reached this level, you will begin to see swirls of color, see mental pictures, or internally hear a voice talking to you. Take note, and keep a journal of any impressions. Come back to normal consciousness by visualizing the colors in reverse sequence.

MEDIUM

A *medium* is a person who has developed their psychic or spiritual awareness to the point where they can act as a go-between from the spiritual realms to the physical realm. There are different types of mediums, ranging from conscious channelers to trance mediums. Some mediums are clairvoyant, while other mediums are clairaudient or clairsentient. Some trance mediums are capable of materializations (*see* MATERIALIZATION and CLAIRVOYANCE), while other trance mediums give you a "past life" reading.

How does a medium acquire this gift? Well, some are born naturals, while others must sit in a development class for years to hone their skills. A medium is something like a television set. You can tune in to invisible frequencies in the air. Without the set, we cannot see pictures. Without the medium, a lot of us cannot communicate with the spirit realms.

METAPHYSICS

Meta, from the Greek, means "after"; and *physics,* means "nature, the science of natural bodies." So, *metaphysics* is that science which seeks to trace the branches of human knowledge to their first principle, or to find what is the nature of the human mind and its relations to the external world. The science of metaphysics seeks to understand the ultimate ground of being . . . or what it is that really exists—embracing both psychology and ontology (the doctrine of "being").

Comment: I believe it was the philosopher Descartes who said: "I think; therefore, I am." I'm not sure; I only secured a "D" standing in that philosophy course. It seems, however, that mankind has always asked these questions since time began: Who am I? Where do I fit in? What is my purpose for being here? What is life all about?

Some people take a lifetime to answer these questions; some don't bother; some are not satisfied with the answers.

Am I part of God? Is God a part of me? Is my purpose for living here and now, a lesson—so I will learn to progress spiritually, that I may once again walk with my Father?

MIND

The term *mind,* especially as used in Buddhism, is not the brain, nor is it physically located somewhere. However, not only is mind "within" us, it is the very essence of what is. Beyond all conceptions, beyond duality, its essence is radiant Awareness, clear space. Its expression is Compassion. Its activity manifests Truth and Wisdom. (*See* MEDITATION.)

Comment: Milton had the basic idea in *Paradise Lost:* "The mind is a place unto itself, and can make a heaven of hell or a hell of heaven."

N

Nostradamus
Numerology

NOSTRADAMUS

Nostradamus was one of the greatest clairvoyants of all time. He was born in France in 1503, and died in 1566. He became a physician and an astrologer. In 1555, he published a book of prophecies entitled *Centuries*. Because of the Church's distrust of fortune tellers and prophets in general, Nostradamus's works are written in a flowery language that disguises many of the predictions. If interpretations of his writings are correct, he accurately predicted: the French Revolution; the rise of Napoleon; the Russian Revolution; the First and Second World Wars; space travel; and many other less important events.

Perhaps his greatest surprise occurred twenty years after his death, when it became necessary to move his tomb. Upon opening it, the workmen found the well-preserved body of Nostradamus; and hanging around his neck, a disc, on which was written that day's date.

NUMEROLOGY

Numerology is the study of numbers. Originally, each letter of the Greek and Hebrew alphabets also stood for a number; therefore, each word represented a number when its letters were added together. In this way, a person's name could be reduced to a number which would bear the characteristics associated with it.

There are two systems for reducing a name to a number, based on the use of the modern, or a mixture of the Hebrew and Greek, alphabets.

In the modern system, the numbers one to nine are used; in the Hebrew—one to eight. The Hebrew method is generally regarded as the most authentic, as the modern letters were never designed to act as numbers.

Values in the Modern Method

1	2	3	4	5	6	7	8	9
a	b	c	d	e	f	g	h	i
j	k	l	m	n	o	p	q	r
s	t	u	v	w	x	y	z	

Values in the Hebrew

1	2	3	4	5	6	7	8
a	b	c	d	e	u	o	f
i	k	g	m	h	v	z	p
q	r	l	t	n	w		
j		s			x		
y							

For example, under the Hebrew method, my name equates to 4.

E l a i n e K a y M u r r a y
5+ 3+ 1+ 1+ 5+ 5+ 2+ 1+ 1 + 4+ 6+ 2+ 2+ 1+ 1= 40
                        4 + 0 = 4

All numbers are reduced to a single number, hence: 40 = 4 + 0 = 4 . . . which corresponds to Uranus.

Each of the planets also has its individual number and, consequently, the person who also bears that number is influenced by them. They are:

Sun = 1
Moon = 2
Jupiter = 3
Uranus = 4
Mercury = 5
Venus = 6
Neptune = 7
Saturn = 8
Mars = 9

* Exceptions: Numbers 11 and 22 are not reduced. These are believed to have their own special characteristics.

When working out a name-number, always use the name by which the person is commonly known; even when this differs from the name with which they were christened.

As well as the name-number, another important number is found from the adding together of a person's birth date. Example:

2 2 of A p r i l   1   9 4 1   You add:

2+ 2 +   1 + 8+ 2+ 1+ 3 + 1+ 9+ 4+ 1 = 34 = 3+4= 7

To interpret your particular number, a further study of numerology would be required.

Critics of numerology point to the fact that names are chosen at random by the parents, before they can know what their child is going to be like. The numerologist answers: Nothing in the universe is left to chance; although the parents may think they are choosing the name, they are simply the agents of cosmic forces.

If the bad points of a number outweigh the good, by changing one's name slightly, or picking a different name altogether, the good aspects of another number can be attracted. If this is done, the old name must be completely forgotten and the new name, or form of spelling, always used.

It is interesting to note how many famous people, especially entertainers, have achieved success after changing their name, and consequently coming under the influence of another number.

Comment: I once heard of some parents whose surname was: Flood. Guess what they named their son? Would you believe "Flash?" That's almost as bad as a boy named "Sue."

O

Occult
Off the Grid
Omnipotent
Oracle
Ouija Board
Over-Soul

OCCULT

Occult means "hidden." That's it. Any practice carried out in secret, hidden from the public, is considered to be *occult*. History tells us that many practitioners of different forms of religion were persecuted, or put to death. Consider the Roman amphitheater where the lions chased the Christians for sport. As a result, many practices became occult in nature.

Today, this word seems to conjure up only negative practices like Satanism. Too many T.V. shows and movies, which deliberately set out to shock and frighten the viewer, have given the word *occult* a bad name.

OFF THE GRID

A new age community term for living without the power company and substituting alternative energy systems.

OMNIPOTENT

Omnipotent means having illimitable power. Since only God is considered to have power without limitation, the word *Omnipotent,* is used to refer to God, and the Cosmos.

ORACLE

The word *oracle* comes from the Latin *orare,* to speak. An oracle can be a place from which prophetic advice is given. An oracle can also be a person who gives prophetic advice.

The great classical Oracle was at Delphi in Greece. The priestess, or Pythoness, sat in a cave on a tripod straddling a cleft in the earth from which arose trance-inducing fumes.

She answered questions put to her by supplicants in a way so ambiguous that misinterpretation led many to ruin.

Oracles of the past appear to have functioned similarly to Spiritualist mediums today.

The oracles became a profiteering industry, and in doing so, gradually lost their power.

Comment: I believe that mediums today, who misuse their power, have their talent (power) taken away. Perhaps this is why so many charlatans have sprung up and spoiled the reputations of many sincere mediums and psychics today.

OUIJA BOARD

A *ouija board* consists of a board with the letters of the alphabet arranged in a circle, together with numbers from 1 - 10, and the words *yes* and *no*. In the center, is a plastic pointer (a planchette), which moves quite easily.

Each player puts a finger on the pointer and asks for a message from the spirits. The pointer then moves round the board, spelling out answers to their questions. You could also use scraps of paper, bearing the letters, and a shiny table, with a wine glass for a pointer.

Using the ouija board differs from a spiritualist séance, because none of the participants have control of the summoned spirit. For this reason, mediums warn against its use, in case the spirit refuses to depart, and attaches itself to one of the players who may or may not become possessed.

Most ouija board players are novices in the field of spiritual communication, so they usually know very little about saying a prayer of protection. Due to their individual belief systems, psychological harm can occur. Of course, the board itself is completely harmless.

One tends to hear only the negative aspects about the ouija board.

OVER-SOUL

Your *over-soul* is the real you. It remains in spirit and sends only a portion of itself to the earth plane, in any one incarnation. The over-soul has collected all the knowledge and experiences from all the incarnations experienced thus far. Some people refer to the over-soul as their higher self. It is certainly much wiser than the earthly portion of itself.

If we can learn to connect with our over-soul or higher self, we can find guidance, purpose, and direction in our daily lives.

P

Palmistry
Paranormal
Parapsychology
Pendulum
Pentagram
Personality
Phenomenon
Pineal and Pituitary Glands
Pleiades
Prayer
Precognition
Premonition
Progression
Projection
Prophet
Protection
P.S.I.
Psychic
Psychic Surgery
Psychokinesis
Psychometry
Pyramids

PALMISTRY

Reading palms, like interpreting the cards or casting a horoscope, is one of the ancient methods of *divination* that is still popular today.

Palmistry is a method of foretelling the future, or stating the past, which is completely personal—as no two palms, like no two fingerprints, are identical.

The palmist begins by looking at the general shape of the hand. There are seven main types:

1. Elementary
2. Square
3. Conical
4. Spatulate
5. Pointed
6. Philosophical
7. Mixed

The texture of the hand is considered next, followed by assessing the thumb and fingers. Each finger is named after a planet, as is the mount or raised fleshy bump at its base. The first finger represents Jupiter; the second—Saturn; the third—Apollo (the sun); and the fourth—Mercury.

From the shape, size, and texture of the hand and fingers, the palmist turns to the lines on the palm. They show the past, future, and personality of the individual. The principle lines of fate, life, head, heart, and fortune should be clearly marked and unbroken. (*See diagram.*)

Lines of Hand
1. Life Line
2. Line of Destiny
3. Line of Fortune
4. Line of Head
5. Line of Intuition
6. Line of Heart
7. Girdle of Venus
8. Line of Mars
9. Rachettes

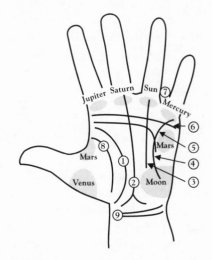

By the clarity and length of these lines, the palmist can deduce the person's future prospects; and how they will be affected by other factors, depending on how they are crossed by smaller lines.

PARANORMAL

The *paranormal* is: anything which is considered to be beyond normal. Any thing which cannot be explained under normal circumstances is *paranormal*. Flying saucers, ghosts, levitation, telepathy, and extrasensory perception are all classified in the category of the paranormal.

PARAPSYCHOLOGY

Parapsychology is a field of research contiguous to, or near, psychology. It concerns such subjects as E.S.P. (extrasensory perception), telepathy, telekinesis, and the phenomena of psychical research. Parapsychology is an empirical approach to such phenomena.

Comment: There are many groups throughout the world today which meet in order to discuss topics of a parapsychological nature.

Laboratory experiments are carefully controlled and impeccable records are kept in order to one day explain that which is unexplained today.

PENDULUM

A *pendulum* is a device for accessing information from the inner self, and using some type of material suspended from a string or a chain. While any material of some weight will do, the best and most responsive pendulum uses a crystal.

Focus your attention on the crystal pendulum and mentally direct it to move back and forth, from side to side, then in a clockwise direction. Lastly, direct it to move in a counterclockwise circle.

When the pendulum moves satisfactorily, you are ready to use your pendulum to detect energy fields. (*Also see* DOWSING.)

PENTAGRAM

The *pentagram* is a symbol sometimes found in church architecture. The five points denote the five wounds of Christ. The use of the symbol, to ward off unwanted spirits from houses, is referred to in the old English song: "Green Grow the Rushes Oh" which contains the line . . . "five for the symbols at your door." (*See diagram.*)

PERSONALITY

The word *personality* pertains to the Inner Man, the Soul, the Psychic, or Divine Being who resides within the physical body. The personality expresses the character of the soul, which has evolved through many cycles of time from the hour of the creation of the soul. The personality reveals all that has been garnered up through numberless experiences and absorbed as part of its very essence of expression. It demonstrates all the qualities which have been adopted by the soul as its own peculiar characteristics or earmarks, so to speak. And so there are all kinds of personalities, according to each individual's evolution. It is due to the personality of the soul, that certain acts or deeds are performed which we recognize as being those performed by a particular personality. The personality reveals the true psychic identity of each individual of the human race.

PHENOMENON

A *phenomenon* is an observable fact or event which is considered remarkable or extraordinary. Usually, someone will wonder why the event happened, and will investigate it. The phenomenon of objects moving, without any apparent cause or assistance, has yet to be explained satisfactorily by the scientific community.

PINEAL AND PITUITARY GLANDS

In their physiological purpose, these glands have to do with the regulating of various functions of the body such as: the circulation of the blood; the growth of the bones and tissues; and the development of the sex and emotional functions. In this sense, they act essentially as governors.

In the psychic sense, the pineal and pituitary glands act like transformers. They step down (for an objective sensing) those exceedingly rapid vibrations which come from the spiritual or psychic planes; or they step up the slower vibrations of a material nature, so that they can be sensed on the immaterial plane.

The pineal and pituitary glands deal so much with the spiritual side of life that it is advisable to develop them slowly. (*See* KUN-DALINI.)

PLEIADES

The *Pleiades* are a brilliant star cluster in the constellation of Taurus. The *Pleiades* are mentioned in many stories and legends. Extraterrestrial encounters have been reported from all over the world and include information that some of the space beings have indicated the *Pleiades* as their place of origin. In the South Pacific, there is a primitive tribe who build saucer-shaped temples in remembrance of their ancestors who (according to legend) came from the stars called *Pleiades*, in saucer-shaped ships.

Comment: During one of my meditations, a being who calls himself *Benjamin Wah* made his presence felt. When I asked him where he was from, he answered (mentally): "From the river in the sky." I interpreted this to mean from some galaxy in space. He was going to aid me in the field of healing. Oddly enough, about the same time, I stumbled across a new age tape, by Gerald Jay Markoe titled: "Music from the Pleiades." Listening to it creates a dreamy, peaceful, "spacy" feeling.

PRAYER

Prayer is a petition, a supplication or entreaty, addressed usually to the Creator, for the granting of some special request. If our prayers are altruistic in nature and purpose, and in harmony with the Divine Scheme, we should hold all confidence that our prayer will be answered.

Comment:
> Ask, and it will be given to you; search, and you will find; knock, and the door will be opened to you. For the one who asks always receives; the one who searches always finds; the one who knocks will always have the door opened to him. Is there a man among you who would hand his son a stone when he asked for bread? Or would hand him a snake when he asked for a fish? If you, then, who are evil, know how to give your children what is good, how much more will your Father in heaven give good things to those who ask him!
>
> Matthew 7:7-11, The Jerusalem Bible

PRECOGNITION

Precognition is to know, beforehand, an event or state, not yet experienced.

Comment: At one time, I taught music at two different elementary schools in Ontario. Because I travelled on my lunch hour, I used to assign two grade seven boys to return a piano from the music room to the foyer outside the principal's office. This was done each noon hour, after lunch, and supervised by the home-room teacher. This saved me about five minutes in travelling time, to get to the other school. This system worked well for many months. One day, out of the blue, I had a very uneasy feeling about the piano. I stopped, dead in my tracks, halfway down the hall, and returned to the music room. I specifically instructed the home-room teacher to BE SURE and supervise the moving of the piano—because boys can be careless. Then I went on my way, putting the entire issue out of my mind. The next day, when I returned, I found out that somehow the boys were not supervised; they had upset the piano on its back, in the middle of the hall. No one was hurt. A case of precognition?

PREMONITION

A *premonition* is: a warning given beforehand. I had a premonition about the safe transport of a piano on a specific day (*see* PRECOGNITION). I acted on this premonition and warned the home-room teacher. She, however, did not follow up on the warning. Hence, the piano was upset in the hallway. It is fortunate that there were no small children in the hallway at the time of the accident; they could have been injured. So, if we pay attention to our premonitions, we can often avoid some grief in our lives.

PROGRESSION

Progression, in new-age terms, means: the spiritual development of the soul. As we experience each incarnation on the earth plane, we have the opportunity to make progress on our journey towards at-one-ment with God. When we have progressed to a certain point, we say our souls are more highly evolved.

PROJECTION

A *projection*, in new-age terminology, generally refers to an astral projection. (*See* ASTRAL PROJECTION.) We can also project our *thoughts* elsewhere.

Comment: I know a lady reverend who used to work with absent healings. She would tell any patient she knew, who was scheduled for surgery, that she would pray for them . . . and be thinking about them. So strong were her thought forms, the patients would often report seeing this lady, standing in the operating room, along with the doctors and nurses. Was it a thought form? Was it an astral projection?

PROPHET

A *prophet* is someone who can foretell future events. A prophet is considered to be inspired or instructed by God to announce these future events. Because the prophet's words and instructions were from God, the people listened and considered their words seriously.

Comment: When Jonah was instructed by Yahweh to "go to Nineveh, the great city, and preach to them as I told you to," we are told that "the people of Nineveh believed in God; they proclaimed a fast and put on sackcloth, from the greatest to the least." Hence, when God saw their efforts to renounce their evil behavior, God relented; he did not inflict on them the disaster which he threatened. (Jonah 3; New Jerusalem Bible.)

PROTECTION

Everyone wants to feel protected. It makes us feel safe in a world where it is becoming less safe each day.

I know two ways to seek protection.

Firstly, you can begin your day by praying to God for protection, and trust your guardian angel to look after you.

Secondly, you can visualize a white light forming a ring of protection around you, your loved ones, your car, house, and place of work. The white light of protection will repel any negative forces. It is also important to keep your thoughts as positive as you can. Like attracts like.

Comment: If you are meditating or playing with a ouija board, it is always wise to say a prayer of protection; also ask that only the "highest and the best" be sent to you (i.e. entities of a high order of spiritual evolvement).

P.S.I.

(*See* PSYCHOKINESIS.)

PSYCHIC

The ancient Greek word for soul was *psyche*. That which lies beyond the range of our physical senses, and extends into infinity as Self, and is seemingly inexplicable . . . is characterized as the *divine* and *psychic*.

When we say a person is "psychic," we infer that they can go beyond their physical senses and tap into the spiritual realms. Because they have this ability, we rely on them to give us direction or foretell the future. It is all right to use this crutch for a while; but it is better to learn to listen to your own inner self. Because we have free will, we ultimately choose our own path to the future anyhow.

PSYCHIC SURGERY

By concentrating the flow of crystalline energies to the hands with great intensity, it allows the psychic surgeon to part the molecular structure of the skin of the subject. The hand of the psychic surgeon literally enters the body cavities. It is comparable to the hand serving as a laser, a fine pinpoint of energy or light. When the surgeon has completed his work, he removes his hand and the skin goes back together, just as easily as we might dip our hand into a basin of water and remove it again.

Comment: If you want to have a good laugh, read Shirley MacLaine's book *Going Within,* chapter 15. She tells about a personal experience with the Reverend Alex Orbito, a psychic surgeon from Manila. It's one thing to read about psychic surgery—it's another to experience it for yourself.

These psychic surgeons remove tumors, etc. from the body, without the aid of a knife, and return the opening to normal, as if nothing were disturbed in the first place.

PSYCHOKINESIS

Psychokinesis is the movement of physical objects through the power of the mind, without use of physical means. There are psychics who claim to have this ability. Uri Geller is probably the most famous . . . or infamous, depending on your point of view. Uri could allegedly make the hands on a clock move, without touching the clock. He also claimed to bend metal objects to the point of breaking, using only mental power.

Poltergeist activity is sometimes attributed to the unconscious psychokinetic powers of adolescents.

PSYCHOMETRY

Psychometry in the psychic world concerns the ability to pick up another person's vibrations by handling or touching something which belongs to the person involved. Mental pictures form in the psychic's mind which pertain to the person who is "being read."

Almost everyone can learn to do psychometry to a small degree if they practice. Professional psychics who have this ability are often called in on police matters. It might involve a murder or a missing person. Often the psychic is successful, while ordinary avenues are not.

Every object retains the impressions of everything that takes place in its vicinity.

Comment: I once purchased an abalone ring while visiting Barbados. For fun, I gave it to a friend of mine to hold, when I returned from the island. I didn't tell her it was a recent acquisition.

"That's the funniest thing," she said. "All I can see is black people."

Then I told her where I got the ring. I had not owned it long enough for my vibrations to influence it. I felt my friend's psychometric abilities were pretty accurate.

Another time, a teacher friend gave me her ring to hold for a reading. Immediately, I broke into tears and sobbed for nearly two minutes before I could bring myself under control. I recognized, of course, that the tears were not mine . . . but were my friend's. I felt her problem was of a marital nature, and that her husband had been unfaithful to her. I was accurate. The story has a happy ending; they worked things out, and are still together today.

Another time, I held the ring from a male teacher who was on our staff. I immediately started giggling. I could see him chasing a greased pig. He laughed in return, and told me it was something he did on a regular basis when he was a little boy.

If you decide to develop your psychometry, please be careful to have a positive attitude; and never tell something to someone that is not helpful in nature.

PYRAMIDS

Pyramids have been constructed in many areas of the world. They are different shapes and sizes, but the most famous pyramids are probably the three large pyramids located at Giza, just outside of Cairo. They are:

1. The Great Pyramid, called *Cheops* by the Greeks. It is associated with King Khufu. Its base covers an area large enough to hold ten football fields (13 acres). Each block weighs two and one-half tons on the average; and each is polished to one, one-thousandth of an inch, fitting so closely, a knife blade cannot be slipped between them.

2. The tomb for King Khafre (Chephren). It has a Sphinx beside it.

3. The tomb for King Menkaure (Myceinus).

Why were the pyramids built? Were they just gigantic tombs built for kings? And how were they built? There are many theories.

One theory suggests the pyramids were built to maintain communication and to open channels with our brothers and sisters in space. The pyramids were used to channel collected energies to, and from the ships, as well as from the energy vortexes (see VORTEXES) emanating from the grid systems. The pyramids were built through the process of levitation.

This is an interesting theory, especially given the fact that the location of the pyramids not only divides the continents and oceans into two equal halves; it also lies at the center of gravity of the continents.

Is it a coincidence that the height of the pyramid of Cheops multiplied by a thousand million—98,000,000 miles—corresponds approximately to the distance between the earth and the sun? Is it a coincidence that the area of the base of the pyramid divided by twice its height gives the celebrated figure π = 3.14159?

Some years ago, a company manufactured miniature pyramids to enclose used razor blades. The energy from the pyramids seemed to sharpen the blades.

Pyramid energy is also accredited for the ability to preserve (mummify) any fruit, or flesh, when it is placed under a pyramid shape. A pyramid shape placed over growing plants, appears to enhance their growth.

Comment: While in Cairo (1963), my brother and myself rode camels out to the Great Pyramid. We crawled through a passageway to the King's Chamber.

I remember feeling a sense of peace, and coolness, after the external temperature of 108° F.

Q

Qabbalah
Quest

QABBALAH

(See KABALA)

QUEST

To go on a *quest,* is to go on a search for something of great value.

There are many *quest* stories throughout history, but the greatest quest is a spiritual one. At the end of a spiritual quest, you find yourself . . . and God, the greatest treasure of all. The spiritual quest need not take you on a pilgrimage to a great city, or a shrine. The journey begins by going within yourself.

R

Rainbow Body
Ramtha
Reflexology
Reiki
Reincarnation
Rolfing
Rosicrucians
Runes

RAINBOW BODY

A phenomenal ability to dissolve the human body into rainbow light leaving only hair, clothing, and nails behind. Enlightened Tibetan masters have been seen by disciples performing this pinnacle of yogic accomplishment and liberation.

RAMTHA

Ramtha is a 35,000-year-old entity channeled by J.Z. Knight of Washington state. Ramtha calls himself the "Enlightened One." Ramtha claims to have incarnated 35,000 years ago as a spiritual and political leader known as "The Ram" who came from Lemuria into what is now India. By using the instrument J.Z. Knight, Ramtha can communicate his philosophy clearly, and effectively. There are several books written on the subject, should you wish to investigate further. (*Also see* CHANNELING.)

REFLEXOLOGY

Reflexology is the science of manipulation of specific reflexes in the hands and feet which correspond to all the glands, organs, and parts of the body. It helps to normalize the body and reduce stress.

Comment: I have had several reflexology sessions. Each time, the sore spots on my feet corresponded to a problem I had somewhere in my body. I still find that amazing.

REIKI

Reiki is an ancient Japanese healing art which uses your hands to channel Universal Life Energy to treat four levels of being: body, mind, emotions, and spirit.

REINCARNATION

Reincarnation is the belief that each of us lives a series of lives. It is an ancient belief, and by no means exclusive to the Eastern religions, in which it forms a central theme.

The Christian teaching that life is a testing period, followed by a once and for all judgment . . . is unacceptable to many.

How, one asks, can a good God, a father, condemn his children to eternal damnation on their record in such a brief flash of time as a single earthly life? What of those born mentally or physically handicapped? What of the baby who dies a few weeks after birth? What of primitive peoples brought up to accept values completely opposite to what civilization in general defines as right and wrong?

Man is part of nature, and nature works in cycles of life, death, and re-birth . . . so why should man be any different?

The idea of reincarnation is far more plausible. Man's purpose is to be reunited with God; but confused by his own free will, he frequently takes a wrong turning; yet with every life he gets a little nearer to the end of the road.

Between lives, the spirit rests and receives instruction from higher beings. It learns where it went wrong so that things can be put right next time, and its development continues.

This "putting right" is the basis for the law of Karma, whereby all actions and thoughts bring their own reward or punishment to the person concerned.

After rest and instruction, the spirit returns to earth as the child of parents and in an environment chosen so that karmic problems can be worked out.

Many believers in reincarnation claim that one of Jesus' missions was to spread the idea of reincarnation to new lands. They interpret Christ's teachings that the sins of the fathers will be visited on the children, as a reference to the law of Karma. His use of the words, "Thy sins are forgiven thee," when healing the sick, suggests that illness and affliction in one life is the punishment for sins in another. Some claim that in saying his "Father's house has many mansions," Jesus was showing that in the one life of the spirit, there are many earthly lives.

Child prodigies are also put forward as further proof of reincarnation. Prodigies are explained by the fact that each of us develops a particular talent over the course of many lives, until it becomes so strong that it manifests itself at an early age.

The knowledge of previous lives is stored deep in the subconscious so that it does not interfere with the present incarnation. This knowledge can be revealed through hypnosis, meditation, and channeling.

Comment: I once attended a session with a trance medium from Scotland. She gave past-life readings. Curiously enough, she described eighteen different lives I had lived throughout history, giving the country where I lived, the sex, circumstances of birth, age, and cause of death. This reading seemed to explain to me the reason for my deep attachment to horses, and my love for flamenco music.

ROLFING

Rolfing is a slow, very deep, manipulative technique used on the body to release tension and trauma held in deep tissue layers.

ROSICRUCIANS

Christian Rosenkreuz is credited with being the founder of the Rosicrucians in the fifteenth century. This society still exists in various forms throughout the world today.

Rosenkreuz travelled throughout the East learning many secrets. He shared his knowledge with three friends upon his return to Germany. Four other people were later admitted to the society, but it was agreed it should remain secret until the world was ready for their revelations.

Those revelations came in 1614 with the publication of *Fama Fraternitatis (Discovery of the Fraternity)*. The context of *Fama Fraternitatis* came from the writings of Rosenkreuz, which were found in his seven-sided tomb beside his perfectly preserved body. This discovery came almost one hundred twenty years after his death (1486) at the age of one hundred and six.

The Rosicrucians is a humanitarian movement, allowing for greater health, happiness, and peace in the earthly lives of all mankind. Their purpose is to enable men and women to live clean, normal, natural lives, as Nature intended, while enjoying all the privileges of Nature.

Rosicrucian members are students and workers, unselfish servants of God to mankind, efficiently educated, trained, experienced, attuned with the mighty forces of the Cosmic or Divine Mind, and masters of matter, space and time. There are no benefits or rights. All members are pledged to give unselfish service, without either hope or expectation of remuneration, to "evolve the Self."

The Rosicrucian cross is gold, with distinctive looped ends. There is one red rose in the center of the cross which is a symbol of Immortality and Reincarnation. (*See* CROSS for a diagram.)

RUNES

Runes is an ancient method of divination for personal instruction. It was believed that by consulting the appropriate rune, you could make contact with the force in nature which the symbol represented, thereby drawing you closer to the gods and aiding you in ordinary day-to-day living. These powerful symbols were carved on many items to influence the weather, to aid the crops, and to heal the sick. These symbols can change in meaning, depending on the perspective of the interpreter. Each must discover a personal runic interpretation by using meditation, dreams, and listening to the inner voice.

It is best to make your own runes out of a natural material such as stone, clay, or wood. They can be round, oval, or oblong, but they should be small enough so that all 25 will fit in the palms of your cupped hands. The symbols can be carved, painted on, or drawn with a felt-tip pen. You will need a bag (also made of natural materials) to carry your runes and a plain cloth on which to spread them. Carry them with you for a while to attune the runes to your personal vibration before seriously attempting an actual divination. You will need a guide book to help you become familiar with the meanings of the symbols and the methodology of doing a runecast.

The runes should never dictate your actions but rather allow you to draw from within solutions to your problems. Runes are a guide to show you what is likely to happen, given your orientation in the world, at the time of the inquiry. There are always variables, and of course "free will." Always listen to your inner voice. Keep notes on each divination because you will be able to see those events come to pass which were foretold weeks, or even months earlier. The runes can be a powerful force; used properly they will enlighten you and help you along life's path.

Use them wisely. (*See diagram of Germanic Rune Symbols.*)

Germanic Rune Symbols

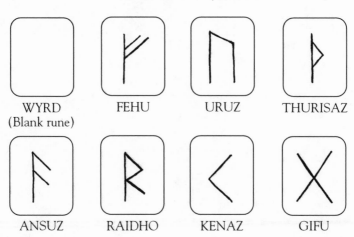

| WYRD (Blank rune) | FEHU | URUZ | THURISAZ |
| ANSUZ | RAIDHO | KENAZ | GIFU |

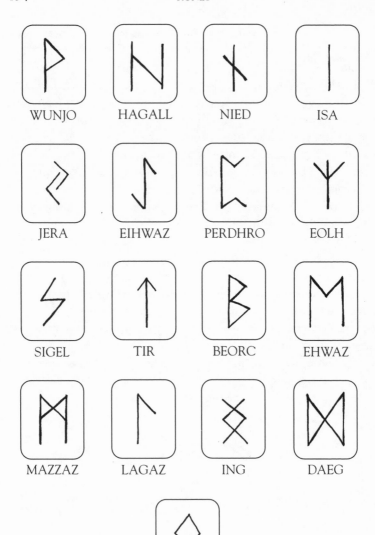

WUNJO HAGALL NIED ISA

JERA EIHWAZ PERDHRO EOLH

SIGEL TIR BEORC EHWAZ

MAZZAZ LAGAZ ING DAEG

OTHEL

S

Séance
Seer
Shaman
Silver Cord
Smudging
Solar Plexus
Sorcerer
Soul
Soul-mate
Spirit
Spiritualism
Spiritualist Philosophy
Star Child
Star Light Elixirs
Stigmata
Subconscious
Sufi
Superconscious
Swami
Sweat Lodge

SÉANCE

A *séance* is the gathering of a group of people for the purpose of communication with the spirit realms. Often séances were held with the hope of communicating specifically with a loved one who has departed from this earthly plane, and is sorely missed by those who are left behind. Usually a trusted medium is the go-between for the two planes. Because the desire for results is so strong on the behalf of the sitters, many charlatans have entered the séance business. This is unfortunate, because there are many sincere workers.

Séances were a product of the spiritualist movement, but the movie industry has dramatized the séance out of proportion, emphasizing the negative aspects, and capitalizing on people's fear of death in general.

In its proper setting, the séance has proved to be a useful tool. The medium might make use of a cabinet (black curtains, hung in the corner of the room) which aids in collecting the energies. A red light allows visibility of any manifestations. The doorkeeper ensures that the medium will be kept unharmed throughout the session. After the medium has gone into trance, ectoplasm from the medium may form figures, or partial figures from spirit, to communicate with one or more of the sitters.

Before sitting in the circle, it is customary to give your name. This is for the purpose of spirit. Apparently there are so many souls clambering to get through, it prepares them on the other side.

You are not supposed to touch these wispy forms since it can do some damage to the medium. However, if these figures touch you, or say "touch me," that is different.

Comment: I have not experienced this type of séance. People who have, assure me that the séance is a valid method of communicating with spirit.

SEER

A *seer* is a person who is capable of "seeing" beyond the five physical senses. Sometimes they are called a "psychic," or a medium. *Seers* could include the prophets of old, and astrologers too. Since the spiritual realms do not operate on a system of time, such as we know it, and the seer has access to these realms, we often get news about future events as well as past events.

We have come a long way from the crystal-ball-toting gypsy fortune tellers, to where we are today. New age thinking demands we take responsibility for ourselves. Don't rely on what some other person says. Ultimately, we have the final choice. If we go "within," we have all the answers for ourselves.

Comment: Easier said than done. There have been some rough times in my life when I couldn't seem to get any answers. It was comforting to go to a respected *seer* and receive some guidance and reassurance for the direction my life should go.

SHAMAN

A *Shaman* is, traditionally, an Indian medicine man or woman who works with spirit influences to heal us when we need it.

Most native cultures have their version of a shaman, whether it be the Huichol Indians of western Mexico, the North American Paiute, the Shoshone of western Nevada, or the Indonesians in the Spice Islands.

A shaman can: inherit power, have it bestowed through a dream, or actively seek it through a quest or apprenticeship.

Most shamans have a "power animal" which comes in spirit form as a teacher, as well as supernatural aid from ghosts of the dead. One shaman might get his power from the hawk that lives in the mountains. Another may get her power from the eagle, otter, or bear.

Prayer is an important part of all shamanism; but it is the shaman's rapport with powerful spirits which gives him power to cure the sick and heal the wounded. The shaman becomes a channel for healing.

The Huichols use the deer spirit to heal. They send it into the body of the sick person. Sometimes the shaman will suck out the illness with a feather. When the illness is sucked out, it comes out in the form of a stone, bone, or worm which is given to the fire or the earth.

Huichol shamanism is a healing tradition: firstly—ourselves; secondly—the family or community; and thirdly—everything upon Mother Earth. Healing involves the body, heart, and spirit. In Huichol tradition, corn represents healing of the body. The deer represents healing of the heart. Peyote represents healing of the spirit.

Fire is very sacred. Huichols say that to become a shaman, you have to learn to communicate with the fire. You learn the fire's language by apprenticing to another shaman. You learn to pray to the spirit of the fire and communicate with it through your heart and spirit. The shaman's job is to give light, like Grandfather fire did in ancient times . . . light to the people, the earth, the world, and all creation.

The Huichol have power places such as caves, the ocean, or a mountain top. In a sacred cave, you learn to communicate with the living being who resides in it. They gain empowerment by fasting and praying in power places. You give a prayer to the place of power, and you get to take back the power of that place.

The Paiute, like others, do not fast when they undertake a vision quest. In fact, when they go to a cave, they might take food for a midnight and morning meal. The aspirant asks for the particular kind of power that he desires.

Power that comes unsolicited makes itself known through repeated dreams. A man may dream that a spirit tells him to be a doctor. The spirit might instruct him to collect certain things, like feathers and a rattle, to be used in doctoring. If any part of the shamanistic paraphernalia, which has been collected at the request of the shaman's spirit, is lost or destroyed, the shaman not only loses his power, but, sickness also results. It is believed that death may follow any other serious breaches of the injunctions placed on the shaman from his spirit instructors.

Ceremonies play an important role in shamanism. During a ceremony, a sacred time and space is entered where past and future are one. Ceremonial work reclaims the spiritual aspect of daily life.

Torajan (Indonesia) healers might use a flute to lure the illness out of the body. A Torajan sword that resembles a machete, with a handle shaped like the horns of a water buffalo, plays an important role in Torajan rituals. These weapons are magical as well as functional. The sword is pressed into various points on the client's neck, shoulders, back, abdomen, thighs, lower legs, and feet. It is pushed into tender spots with apparent force, yet the skin is not broken. Vital Energy is transferred to the client via the shaman's hands, or through the sword. Sliced onions and other herbal remedies are used. Sometimes the shaman charges herbs and holy water with her vital energy, and gives them to her clients as "follow-up medicine," to be taken after the healing session.

Today, non-native people are participating in vision quests, in order to enter shamanic states of consciousness.

Questers go without food and the company of others during their solo time. The vision quest is an initiation process involving death: something almost always dies on the quest—our fears, our limitations, concepts about ourselves, or a worn-out belief system. The vision quest process involves ceremonies with long periods of drumming and rattling to move one into a state of altered consciousness and into the world of spirit. Sometimes a medicine name is received during a quest, but it may take a lifetime of learning about, and growing into, the medicine name.

The Shaman's message is: to love and enjoy life. Go beyond feelings of anger and jealousy to reach God—for balance and harmony in life. Learn to communicate with the land, the ocean, and spirit of the deer. Focus on trying to do things according to the harmony of the laws of nature and life in general. Spiritualize your life.

Comment: We have much to learn from the shamanic way of life.

SILVER CORD

The *silver cord* is that thin strand which connects the physical with the spiritual body. It is elastic in nature and can stretch almost indefinitely. Upon death, the silver cord is completely severed, allowing the physical body to die, while the spiritual body continues to move, think, and have its dimension. People who do astral travelling are quite aware of this silver cord.

SMUDGING

Smudging is a ceremony using smoke to purify the psychic energy of a place or the energy field (aura) around a person. Most often, dried sage, cedar or mugwort is used. At times one or more of these are bound together in a "smudge stick."

SOLAR PLEXUS

The *solar plexus* is one of the most important groups of small plexuses, forming the largest plexus in the human body; located in the center of the abdomen. Its objective or physical functioning is very important; but far more important, is its psychic or sympathetic functioning. It was believed by the ancients that this plexus was the center of the Soul in man, as the sun is the center of the solar world, hence its name. The solar plexus is associated with the third chakra, the color yellow, and is greatly connected to our emotions.

SORCERER

A *sorcerer* is a wizard who is supposed to possess magical powers. Who has not listened to Paul Dukas's "The Sorcerer's Apprentice?" or seen the Walt Disney version, using Mickey Mouse? Sorcerers can be wonderful characters in fiction, but I am told they are not just a product of fantasy: there are people who practice negative "black" magic and who seek to overpower, subdue, or destroy other individuals or things. By their intentions you shall know them.

SOUL

The *soul* is that spiritual part of God which resides inside each human being. This Divine spark is eternal and never dies, even when our physical bodies are dead and buried. It is this Divine spark in each man which connects all of mankind together. We are all a part of God; God is a part of us. Each time we incarnate upon the earth, the soul grows a little wiser, gains a little more experience, progresses a little more. When we evolve enough to become ONE with our Mother/Father/God, it will no longer be necessary for our souls to reincarnate upon the earth.

Comment: I can't believe people can get much out of living if they do not believe in some form of after-life, or the existence of the soul. If there is no soul . . . what would be the point in living?

Whenever my dad and I would get into philosophical discussions about the soul and life-after-death, my mother would pooh-pooh the subject. Her belief in a soul was questionable. However, when she lay on her death bed, I decided it was time for at least one discussion on the subject.

One or two days before mom passed over, I took her a chilled thermos of egg-nog. She seemed to enjoy a few cold sips from the bent straw.

"Mom," I began. This was not going to be easy. "Mom, you are soon going to get rid of this peanut-shell of a body. Do you understand?"

Mom nodded *yes*.

"I know you have never thought much about your spiritual self, but it is important to know what to do. When you pass over and get rid of this peanut-shell, it's important to look for the light. If you go towards the light—there will be someone there to help you . . . maybe even Dad . . . do you understand?"

Again, she nodded *yes*.

"If you go towards the light, everything will be just fine. Don't worry about a thing. You'll be taken care of." I kissed mom on the forehead and told her I loved her; then I left.

At the funeral chapel, I fought back my tears as I was ushered to a front row reserved for family members. All I could think of was: Keep your composure, Elaine. Suddenly, somewhere to the rear, and left, slightly above the heads of the people, I could hear mom call to me.

"Elaine! Elaine. I found the light!" I heard this with my inner ear—but I heard it as clearly as if audibly spoken. A strange calm came over me. Mom was fine. Soon we would bury the peanut-shell; but mom's true self was beginning a whole new experience, free of her diseased body at last.

SOUL-MATE

A spiritual union of two is a blending of a harmonious compatible vibration. This union exists in Love—pure, and without restrictions.

When two souls share this blessed union, it is an additional blessing for them to complete their union in a physical manner (if they wish to).

Comment: There is no greater joy on earth than to find your soul's mate, and share a life together. One compliments and mirrors the other. One begins where the other leaves off. It is a physical, mental, emotional, and spiritual union.

> Joy
> To give love . . . is good,
> To receive love . . . is better;

But to give, and to receive
The gift of love . . .
Is to know exquisite joy.
                    Elaine Murray

SPIRIT

Spirit is not physical. Spirit can reside in or out of the physical, and take on different forms. Because spirit is not physical, it takes a special ability to see spirit. Sometimes it is easier to sense spirit than actually see it. Part of us is spirit. There are also nature spirits, and spirits of departed earth beings. Some say the spirit world is the real world—and the physical world is an illusion.

Comment: As a child, the concept of *spirit* was a difficult one to assimilate. I remember my Sunday school teacher trying to explain that God the Father, God the Son, and God the Holy Spirit were all One. How could they be One, if there were three? My young mind was having a difficult time. Then my teacher took out three wooden matches. She carefully lit one and told me to hold it. Then she lit two more. She gave one to a friend, and held the last match herself. The three matches represented the Father, the Son, and the Holy Spirit. This, I understood. Then she placed all three matches together. They suddenly formed one flame. They were three; yet they were one. I began to understand a little bit about spirit. I'm still working at it to this day.

SPIRITUALISM

The primary objective of *Spiritualism* today is to prove the survival of the human personality after death. Spiritualists attempt to do this through their regular church services. Their services are very similar to many Protestant church services, with the exception of "messages from spirit world" given at the end of the service by a trained medium.

Its adherents believe Spiritualism is a way of life in that it combines philosophy, science, and religion. They generally agree on eight basic principles as follows:

1. We believe in Infinite Intelligence.

2. We believe that the phenomena of nature, both physical and spiritual, are the expression of Infinite Intelligence.

3. We affirm that a correct understanding of such expression, and living in accordance therewith constitute true religion.

4. We affirm that the existence and personal identity of the individual continues after the change called "death."

5. We affirm that communication with the so-called "dead" is a fact, scientifically proven by the phenomena of Spiritualism.

6. We believe that the highest morality is contained in the Golden Rule: "Whatsoever ye would that others should do unto you, do ye also unto them."

7. We affirm the moral responsibility of the individual and that he makes his own happiness or unhappiness as he obeys or disobeys Nature's Physical and Spiritual Laws.

8. We affirm that the doorway to reformation is never closed against any human soul, here or hereafter.

SPIRITUALIST PHILOSOPHY

We have an earthly body and a spiritual body which is linked by a cord.

When we die, the cord linking the physical body and the spiritual body is severed.

There is no hell whose inhabitants are condemned for eternity. Once self-realization dawns and the soul is ready to advance, there are enlightened spiritual beings who will show the way to progress. Heaven and hell are really states of mind.

The world we inhabit after death is round and about us, interpenetrating the world in which we live now. Often our departed loved ones are close by our side, striving to help and guide us, loving us just as they did before passing.

Microphones and radio receivers enable us to hear what is normally beyond the range of our ears. The telescope and television bring into focus what is normally beyond our vision. Inhabitants of the spirit world are very real even though we cannot see or hear them. Highly sensitive individuals who have developed their innate, natural psychic faculties, can tune in to spirit world. These human television and radio sets are mediums. They become the agents through whom spirit communication is achieved.

God is spirit. Wherever there is life, there is spirit; and wherever there is spirit, there is life. We exist because a spark of Divinity is within each one of us. This is a divine relationship in which God is our Father and we are all His children. We can, by our lives, fan the spark into a flame so that a greater expression of Divinity is made known through us. The result will be to sustain, uplift, and help us in our spiritual development. We have the free will to ignore and reject the spark of Divinity.

They regard Jesus as an exemplar, not a savior. Man has no savior but himself.

We are each personally responsible for our sins and must atone for them here and hereafter. We must acknowledge our sins, and try to make amends rather than place them on the shoulders of another.

Jesus was divine—but only in the sense that we are all divine. They believe Jesus developed his psychic faculties and was a supreme master of spiritual law. Jesus was in close touch with the spirit world and demonstrated his survival after his death. His teaching of brotherhood, love, humility, and service is the basis of Spiritualism today.

Some religions preach an after-life as a hope, faith, or belief; the Spiritualist maintains any reasonable person can prove it himself.

Love plus harmony plus peace equals health.

STAR CHILD

A *Star Child* is a person whose soul has experienced many incarnations. They are always here on earth, in service to mankind. They are not used to taking impurities from our atmosphere into their vibrations, consequently Star Children often suffer from sinus conditions, and ear and throat infections. When star children are very young, they seem wise beyond their years.

STAR LIGHT ELIXIRS

A vibrational preparation made by focusing the light of stars into a pure water medium to be taken in a similar fashion to flower essences.

STIGMATA

Stigmata is the physical phenomena of bleeding from parts of the body without any physical injury. These wounds appear on people who exhibit a high religious devotion. The wounds are similar to those of Jesus the Christ. Holes are formed in the palms of the hands, on the soles of the feet, and the side opens as if it had been pierced by a spear. Blood actually flows from these holes. Sometimes small wounds appear on the forehead where Jesus would have worn His crown of thorns.

St. Francis of Assisi received such stigmata, but many thought it was just a legend. Competent scientists have thoroughly investigated cases of stigmata such as that of Padre Pio. The verdict is: stigmata does actually occur, and they emit blood.

Why does stigmata occur? Is it the power of the mind, acting through imagination upon the astral body, which in turn changes the physical body?

SUBCONSCIOUS

I think we all know what being conscious is . . . that's when we are wide awake, and our brains are functional on all levels.

Let someone hit you over the head with a baseball bat, and you become unconscious. Your brain is still functioning on some levels (assuming you are still breathing), but you are no longer in a "conscious" state of mind.

When it comes to the *subconscious*, we really get into trouble, because most of the time we are unaware of it. "Sub" means *under;* so . . . our *subconscious* is just under our conscious attention. Some people refer to our subconscious as our lower self.

Actually our subconscious is more like a computer in nature. It constantly collects data from experiences and stores it away in its memory bank. Our subconscious even stores trivia and junk that we would be better off not possessing. Because our subconscious is like a computer, it cannot think for itself, but tends to react to information and stimuli from previous ideas which we once believed were true. Take your childhood for example. Perhaps your mother told you not to stand in a draft or you would catch a cold. If you were caught in a rainstorm and got wet, then stood in a draft—you would catch a very bad cold. Scientific studies have shown that neither wet clothes, nor a draft, contribute to whether you catch a cold or not. Your conscious mind knows this—but if your subconscious has the childhood program "draft equals cold" stored in its memory banks, chances are: if you're caught in a downpour, then have to ride in a drafty bus to get home—you will catch a cold. So . . . it is important to reprogram our subconscious to our advantage. Tell it positive things like: my body needs to weigh one hundred thirty pounds. I will naturally choose the proper foods to attain my goal.

Just as the subconscious can be used to store positive things, so too can it store some negative stuff. On occasion, this can be a blessing. In cases where someone has been severely abused, the conscious mind cannot deal with the hurt and pain; so the experience is shoved into the subconscious. One woman witnessed her father kill one of her friends, but did not remember the heinous crime until long after she became an adult.

In such negative instances, our subconscious is truly a blessing in disguise. Our subconscious is even capable of creating multiple personalities when a victim's life is particularly unbearable. It may take years of therapy to unlock all the secrets stored in the subconscious and replace this information with positive suggestions and strategies. Only then, can the personalities become integrated, and the person become whole.

Comment: We should be very careful how we program our subconscious. It is very powerful.

SUFI

Sufis are mystics who originated in the Near and Middle East, whose esoteric knowledge and teaching methods have existed for thousands of years. It is thought that they seek to perfect the human mind and heart in such a way as to transcend ordinary human limitation.

SUPERCONSCIOUS

The *superconscious* refers to our higher self. If we function in the conscious mind in our day to day living, and the subconscious is just under our conscious mind, then the superconscious is just above the conscious mind. Through work and awareness, we can find out what is stored in our subconscious. Through meditation and prayer, we can connect with our superconscious. Our higher self is wise; it is the spiritual part of us which is connected to the Divine Intelligence. If we ask our higher selves to guide us in our lives, we are asking that spark of the Divine Creator to help us. Then we have to learn to listen for the answers. We can also program the subconscious to some extent. Express a need and create thought forms to accompany the request. Chances are, the superconscious will manifest that need into reality. (*See* MANIFESTING)

SWAMI

Swami is a Hindu title of respect, equivalent to "master" or "Lord."

SWEAT LODGE

The *sweat lodge* is a Native American ceremonial structure often made of supple willow branches and covered with hides or tarps. The participants sit inside "mother earth" in darkness after hot rocks are placed inside the central firepit. Heat and steam, chanting, singing and prayers accompany healing ceremonies often led by a medicine person. This purification ceremony varies from tribe to tribe.

T

Table Tipping
Talisman
Tao
Tarot Cards
Telekinesis
Telepathy
Theosophy
Thought Forms
Trance
Transcendental
Triangle
Trumpets
Twelve Step Program

TABLE TIPPING

Table tipping is something like using a ouija board for spirit communications. The participants sit in a circle around a small table, placing their finger tips lightly upon it. Soon the table begins to vibrate, and when this vibration reaches a certain intensity, the table begins to move about in a more or less intelligent manner. It can move towards one sitter and caress him, or it may manifest displeasure through violent gyrations. If the control is a certain deceased personality which is mentioned by the sitters, the table may pound violently on the floor. A predetermined method of communication is established (say—one knock for "yes," two knocks for "no"), and the questions can begin.

What makes the table vibrate and thump about? Perhaps it is the unconscious muscular contractions of the sitters which begins the action. Then perhaps the entity uses etheric energy drawn from organic substance (namely the medium and others present). The table becomes so charged with energy as to give the impression of being alive. The table in some instances will levitate completely from the floor, or rock while no fingers are closer than several inches above it. It may even move entirely across the room with no one touching it.

Comment: The teacher for one of the development classes I attended mentioned table tipping. She wondered how many of us had participated in table tipping. A couple of us had not witnessed such a phenomenon, so she requested that a small table be brought into the room. The group of five placed their finger tips on the table. With some gentle persuasion, the table soon began to move. For demonstration purposes, our teacher asked the table to move from the living room to the kitchen. The table began to slowly make its way to the kitchen, sliding as it were, then speeded up. We had fun trying to maintain contact with the table while going through two doorways. When the table reached the kitchen, it stopped dead. You could feel that all energy had drained from the object.

TALISMAN

A *talisman* is anything used for intuitive reasons to bring luck and ward off negative influences or negative energy. Religion, superstition, a ritual, or a ceremony can be involved. A *talisman* can be as simple as a favorite hat or a lucky penny . . . and is thought to amplify, channel, or cause some catalytic process to take place.

TAO

Tao literally means "the way" or the path of life. Taoist philosophy originated in ancient China and teaches balance and the attainment of natural simplicity in all phases of life—cooking, medicine, politics, philosophy, exercise, meditation—and a comprehensive way of "seeing" reality. The most eminent preserved writing is *The Tao Te Ching* by Lao Tzu.

TAROT CARDS

A deck of Tarot cards is a popular tool for divination. The original deck consisted of 78 cards, 56 of which were divided into four suits of swords, cups, coins, and rods . . . while the other 22 bore symbolic pictures.

The origin of the Tarot is obscure; they were likely first used as a divination aid in Persia, then brought into Europe at the beginning of the Middle Ages by the gypsies. Today there are a number of Tarot decks, various "throws" or spreads, and the interpretation of the cards vary from deck to deck.

General Guide to Basic Designs and Usual Definitions:

0. *The Fool.* Design: A jester in a patchwork coat carrying a bundle on a stick across the shoulder and chasing a butterfly near the edge of a cliff over which he is likely to fall.

Meaning: Everything and nothing. The center of the circle. Foolishness and the divine spirit of man. The falling over the cliff represents the entry of the spirit into man.

1. The *Juggler.* Design: A man juggling with balls—sometimes depicted as planets—which he keeps in perpetual motion or standing by a table twirling a baton.
Meaning: The divine power that keeps all things moving and creates everything.

2. *The High Priestess.* Design: A dark-skinned woman seated on a throne between two pillars from which hangs a veil. Sometimes known as the Female Pope.
Meaning: The eternal mother and also the eternal virgin; the veil represents the hymen. She is the sum of all opposites and, as such, represents divine knowledge.

3. *The Empress.* Design: A pregnant, fair-haired, smiling woman accompanied by a sparrow and a dove.
Meaning: The spirit of nature and of love. Birth and rebirth.

4. *The Emperor.* Design: A king holding a scepter.
Meaning: Worldly power and the material side of life. Ambition.

5. *The Pope.* Design: A Pope giving the papal blessing and holding a set of keys.
Meaning: Spiritual power and development.

6. *The Lovers.* Design: A young couple with a child, or . . . a man choosing between two women.
Meaning: Love and innocence. The reconciliation of opposites.

7. *The Chariot.* Design: A warrior in a chariot drawn by two horses, one white and one black.
Meaning: Spiritual progress. The command of the opposing forces of nature.

8. *Justice*. Design: A woman holding scales and a sword.
Meaning: The balancing of power. The reasoning force of the individual.

9. *The Hermit*. Design: An old man carrying a lantern and a staff.
Meaning: Inner vision which guides others.

10. *Wheel of Fortune*. Design: A seven-spoked wheel and an angel.
Meaning: The endless circle of the seasons and of incarnation and reincarnation.

11. *Strength*. Design: A woman closing the jaws of a lion.
Meaning: Spiritual strength and discipline.

12. *The Hanged Man*. Design: The man hangs upside down, suspended by one leg, from the gallows. Sometimes he carries two bags of gold.
Meaning: Self-awareness through the shedding of material values.

13. *Death*. Design: A skeleton with a scythe reaping a field of human heads. Sometimes hands and legs are growing in their place.
Meaning: Death and rebirth.

14. *Temperance*. Design: A man pouring a liquid from one cup to another.
Meaning: Changes and transformations.

15. *The Devil*. Design: The devil holding a man and a woman on a chain.
Meaning: Ambition and lust for power.

16. *The Tower Struck By Lightning*. Design: A tower surmounted by a crown crumbling, after being struck by lightning.
Meaning: Death and destruction. The demolishing of hope and pride.

17. *The Stars*. Design: A naked girl pours water from two ewers into a pool or stream.
Meaning: Spiritual aspiration that brings all things together.

18. *The Moon*. Design: Drops of blood fall from a moon onto a path that leads between two towers.
Meaning: Initiations and new beginnings. The entry into a new world of the spirit.

19. *The Sun*. Design: Two children playing in the sunshine.
Meaning: The beginning of the growth of intellect and spiritual powers.

20. *Judgment*. Design: A picture of the Day of Judgment with an angel summoning the dead from their graves.
Meaning: A desire for better things, of new chances and the fulfillment of aspirations.

21. *The World*. Design: A naked woman dancing in a bed of flowers.
Meaning: Release. The first step of a progress that will lead to realization.

A person who wishes to consult the Tarot cards, shuffles the symbol cards and spreads them face down on a table. He then selects thirteen cards which are then interpreted according to their relationship to each other.

TELEKINESIS

(*See* PSYCHOKINESIS.)

TELEPATHY

Telepathy is the apparent communication from one mind to another, without the use of the senses.

We utilize the frontal areas of the brain, in conjunction with the spiritual third eye, to achieve this process.

Draw in energy through the crown chakra. Allow it to flow to the frontal lobes of the brain and out through the third eye. By using this method, you are capable of sending thoughts and images to others.

To receive information, simply reverse the process. Draw the energy in through the third eye to those areas of the brain, and the understanding will come to the mind.

Comment: We all experience telepathy to some degree. How many times have you and a friend said something simultaneously? How many times have you thought of someone, only to have the telephone ring and find that person on the other end of the line?

THEOSOPHY

The Theosophical Society was formed in New York by Helena Blavatsky, Colonel H.S. Olcott, and William Q. Judge in 1875. Its headquarters were set up at Madras.

The main objective of the Theosophists is to reconcile orthodox Christian beliefs, Eastern mysticism, and the occult.

Theosophists believe in the process of reincarnation and karma, and the gradual reconciliation of the spirit with God through the leading of pure lives and attaining divine knowledge.

Leaders of the theosophy movement believed they were guided by powerful teachers and masters from spirit. By spreading their philosophy, they believed they could bring man to a greater understanding of his world and his destiny. (*See* BLAVATSKY)

THOUGHT FORMS

Thought forms are artificially created forms, either consciously or unconsciously, by those on the physical plane. They fade away when the intensity of the emotion and power that created the forms diminishes.

Visualization is another dimension of thought forms. Our thoughts are very powerful and should be used for positive results only. Cancer clinics and other centers which treat the incurably ill are using positive thinking and visualization skills to prolong life, and in some cases permit a total remission of the life-threatening disease.

Using meditative techniques, we can decrease our oxygen consumption in just ten minutes to a level which is seventeen percent lower than the amount used after six to seven hours of sleep. A cardiac patient can reduce his heartbeat by three beats per minute.

The metabolic level shows a marked decrease during meditation, indicating a state of deep body rest. This reduces stress—probably our number one killer. All these changes can be brought about . . . but they must begin with the thought form, before the results can be manifested.

Comment: As you think—so you become. So be careful how you think!

TRANCE

A *trance* is an altered state of consciousness whereby information from the spiritual plane is relayed to the physical plane. (*See* BRAIN WAVE FREQUENCIES; CAYCE, EDGAR; CHANNELING; CIRCLES; *and* SÉANCE.)

TRANSCENDENTAL

Transcendental means the act of rising above physical and material limitations of life into those realms of pure inspiration and aspiration which can cause man to become anything he dreams of becoming.

Transcendental Meditation is a Yoga-related technique popularized by the former Beatle guru, Maharishi Mahesh Yogi.

In TM the "guru" or teacher gives each of his "chelas," or students, his or her own mantram.

Medical science tells us we only use between five and ten percent of our mind's potential. Through regular meditation, we can realize and utilize a greater portion of our mind and our creativity.

TRIANGLE

The *triangle* was a mystical and powerful figure long before it was adopted by the early Christian church to symbolize the Trinity.

In Christian belief, the triangle represents God, Christ, and the Holy Spirit which is similar to its ancient interpretation as God, man, and the divine spark which connects both.

The Star of David, which combines two triangles to form a six-pointed star, was believed to be especially potent as a symbol of protection.

TRUMPETS

Trumpets are like collapsible funnels with the small end being an inch or so in diameter, while the large end might be nine inches to one foot across. They collapse for storage purposes. These extended trumpets are placed on the floor during a séance, or during a development class session when students sit for a meditation in the Spiritualist Church. When the power is very strong, these trumpets are said to float in the air while spirit uses them to amplify their voice. This way communication from spirit can be facilitated. Because most sittings occur in the dark, a ring of luminous paint is generally applied to both ends. That way, if the trumpet moves, everyone can see it.

Comment: In my experience with trumpets and development classes, spirit never once picked up the trumpet. (They tell me it was more common years ago.) One night, when the apports occurred (*see* APPORTS), the trumpet collapsed into a small heap on the floor, scaring some of the group half to death. I think it would have been very interesting to observe and hear a manifestation which used the trumpet.

TWELVE STEP PROGRAM

The *Twelve Step Program* is a systematic recovery program designed to help people addicted to alcohol live a happy, healthy life of sobriety. The program, based on a belief in a higher power, is used at Alcoholics Anonymous (AA) meetings, as well as other addiction related support and recovery groups.

U

Ultra-sensitive
Undines
Universal Law
Universal Mind

ULTRA-SENSITIVE

An *ultra-sensitive* is an emotionally multi-faceted person who senses the subtle realms of existence, both emotionally and intuitively. The many types of ultra-sensitives, according to Marcy Calhoun in *Are You Really Too Sensitive?*, operate either in a structural or conceptual way. *Structural ultra-sensitives* deal with details first before creating a structure, and *conceptual ultra-sensitives* work with whole concepts or overviews before being concerned with details. *Feeling ultra-sensitives* "pick up" information through their feelings, sometimes not knowing when their emotional or physical pain belongs to themselves or someone else. *Visual ultra-sensitives* receive information in their mind's eye and can visualize people, places or things that aren't physically present. *Knowing ultra-sensitives* just *know*, beyond a shadow of a doubt, without knowing how or why. *Auditory ultra-sensitives* can intuitively hear beyond the words that people are saying.

An ultra-sensitive can be all four of these types and within these four types there are the following seven categories. *Bridge ultra-sensitives* have the ability to network and bridge people, thoughts and innovative ideas and projects. *Catalyst ultra-sensitives*, by their very presence, allow others to create movement and change in their lives. *Sponge ultra-sensitives* totally absorb information and feel, know, see and hear it as their own personal experience or information until they learn to differentiate between "self" and "other." *Vessel ultra-sensitives* selectively absorb only from people they have a personal interest in or are connected to in either a positive or negative way. *Negative potential ultra-sensitives* are not negative people but have a tendency to see only the negative or positive extremes. *Blocked ultra-sensitives* are people who are blocked emotionally or intuitively from information that would help them to live a fuller, richer life. *Multi-talented* (or multi-faceted) *ultra-sensitives* are people with all the above mentioned gifts. Since ultra-sensitives have such a deep understanding and empathy for other people, with proper guidance, they make excellent teachers, counselors and healers of all kinds.

UNDINES

Undines is a more classical name for water spirits or fairies. (*See* FAIRIES)

UNIVERSAL LAW

Universal Laws are decreed by the Divine Mind. These laws operate alike on all planes, and are extremely simple.

The purpose of Universal Law is to ensure progressive gradations or cycles of evolution in spite of all the obstacles placed by man to thwart their operation. The motive behind Universal Law is the preservation of life for the attaining of the ideal expression, or enlightenment. This goal recognizes no man-made ideal, no man-made law, no dictates of civilization where these are contrary to the best purposes as decreed by the Divine Mind.

Universal Law is always constructive, even when it seems destructive. Some Universal Laws include the following:

You shall not impose yourself on another individual; nor shall you inflict your vibrations upon those of another.

Like attracts like.

When an action is taken, and it is taken in your truth, there is no karma involved.

When a soul is involved in an incarnation of voluntary service for God, and in the course of that incarnation does not fulfill the obligations of the contract, the contract itself automatically becomes renewed.

UNIVERSAL MIND

The *Universal Mind* is the consciousness of God and pervades all space in the universe. It also pervades all living beings on the earth plane.

V

Veda
Vessel
Vision Quest
Vital Life Force
Vortex

VEDA

The Veda is the sacred literature of the Hindus and the oldest literature of India, originally preserved by oral tradition. The Veda is any of four ancient books consisting of psalms, chants, ritual formulas, and commentaries called Upanishads, the beginnings of Hindu philosophy.

VESSEL

A vessel is the human body. The soul creates the body in accordance with earth-plane laws, in order to provide a "house" for itself. By entering the denser, physical dimension, the soul can work on perfecting the lessons it has set out to learn. Progression is the result.

When a medium or channel steps aside (mentally) and allows a spiritual entity to use the body to communicate, the word vessel is also used.

VISION QUEST

See SHAMAN.

VITAL LIFE FORCE

Vital Life Force refers to that form of energy which vitalizes the human body at the moment of birth, and leaves the human body at the moment of transition. The vital life force is from the same source as all energy, but is of a distinct and different rate from that which constitutes spirit energy and soul energy.

Some healers are capable of channeling vital life force into their sick patients—giving the patient a boost towards perfect health. There is a Chinese discipline which teaches us how to direct this vital life force for ourselves (*see* CHI).

VORTEX

There is a magnetic grid system covering the surface of this planet. Vortexes are like exit points for magnetic energy to flow back and forth. Some theorize that this magnetic grid system is used by spaceships travelling from vast distances to the vortexes where the ships will function at a different vibrational level.

If you are able to locate an energy vortex, and stay within its area for a period of time, you will notice the difference in the force of the energy. You may feel light-headed, because for a few brief moments, you are involved in the aspects of spiritual time, not Earth physical time.

For the past several years, the vortexes have been shifting in location. The reason is to draw the Children of Light to other, more concentrated areas, so that they may build a unification among themselves.

W

Walk-in
White Brotherhood
White Light
Wisdom

WALK-IN

A *Walk-in* is an entity which takes over the body of one who wishes to depart, instead of being born as an infant. This is always done with permission. The Walk-in first completes the task of the body's previous owner, before it launches on its own projects. A Walk-in's role is like that of a gardener who plants seeds on the planet, helps those seeds to germinate, and then allows them to grow in their own direction.

The Walk-in is a superior soul, but not a perfected soul, and has undergone many earthly lives. Such a soul wishes to avoid returning to the earth plane as a baby and wasting the unneeded learning time of childhood. A Walk-in will take over (with permission) the body of a discouraged soul who wants to leave, or cannot keep their body alive.

Some Walk-ins are unaware that they were not always in the bodies they now inhabit, because they inherit the memory bank of the Walk-out.

According to Ruth Montgomery, Walk-ins are trying to bring a modicum of intelligence to those groping in the dark for solutions to the world's ills. Many Walk-ins work to release those who regret having chosen this period in which to incarnate. Their main mission is to help humankind as servants of the Creator.

The soul exchange often occurs while the body is asleep.

A Walk-in has earned the right, through many lifetimes of spiritual growth, to return directly to the earth plane as an adult. A Walk-in takes over an unwanted body. Sometimes the original occupant becomes depressed and wishes to bow out. In other cases, an accident or severe illness has damaged the body to such an extent that its inhabitant can no longer maintain the spark of life.

All Walk-ins are filled with a sense of purpose. Some are trying to improve people's health through a greater understanding of herbs and sound nutrition. Some are working to help dispel the fear of death. Others are establishing self-reliant communities that can function without electricity and modern technology. (This is in response to a predicted shift of the earth on its axis.) Still others are working to foster more creative and harmonious ways to solve problems of human interactions.

Comment: I have met one person who claims to be a Walk-in. She is a lady who gave readings at a psychic fair in Kelowna British Columbia. She enhanced her readings by drawing pictures using melted crayons as her medium. As well as giving the readings, she had a stack of books for sale. I was prompted to buy one of her books, only to learn that the lady claimed to be a Walk-in from another planet. She had been a "he" on this other planet, and found the adjustment quite trying. The transfer of souls occurred when a female plunged down a stairwell to her death, and the new soul took over. The Walk-in related in her book what it was like when "he" lived on the other planet. She also related to us, verbally, past recollections of her current life (an inheritance of a memory bank?). She was currently remarried and forging ahead with a new sense of direction.

I believe I truly did meet a Walk-in.

WHITE BROTHERHOOD

A group of beings dedicated to helping the earth and its inhabitants reach a higher level of consciousness. Some of these beings are embodied on earth and others work from other realms.

WHITE LIGHT

White light is used for healing and as a method of protection, as when we surround ourselves with the white light. When white light is refracted through a prism, all of the other colors become visible. Each of these colors serve a purpose as well.

White light is associated with the "Divine Light" and other spiritual entities.

WISDOM

Wisdom is the understanding, or the ability to apply knowledge. Knowledge is an accumulation of particular facts and ideas, whereas wisdom is judgment in exercise of the knowledge had. Wisdom may cause the rejection of previously acquired knowledge.

Some students acquire knowledge for years, but they never learn wisdom. Some very wise people have very little formal learning.

Comment: Remember King Solomon who was supposedly very wise? Do you remember his solution to his problem when two women both claimed to be the mother of a certain baby?

I believe the Bible also tells us to "go to the ant, thou sluggard; consider her ways and be wise." (Proverbs 6:6)

X

X

X

X stands for the unknown. In algebra, we are taught to let the unknown quantity = "x."

When x-rays were first discovered, the rays were not fully understood; so they became "x" rays. The name sticks to this day.

When people did not know how to write their name, they were permitted to sign with an x, provided it was witnessed. Today, when we are asked to fill out any of a multitude of forms which x-ist in the world of business, they still mark the signature spot with an "x" and tell you to sign.

Perhaps the form of the X is a throw back to the ancient runic symbol where "x" indicates a partnership of some sort . . . either in business or in love.

XP are the first two letters in the Greek word for "Khristos," thus X has become a symbol or emblem for Christ.

Hurrah for X-mas holidays!

And, as a child, did you not sign your home-made mother's day cards with OOO's and XXX's?

Y

Yahweh
Yoga
Yogi

YAHWEH

Yahweh comes from the verb "to be" and is considered to be the personal name of God. In the Bible, this personal name is the Tetragrammaton, or name of four letters: YHVH, and considered too sacred to be spoken aloud.

The Jerusalem Bible uses the word *Yahweh* throughout its text.

YOGA

Yoga is an ancient Hindu system of self-discipline and training designed to unite body, mind, and spirit through exercise, breathing, and meditation. The first writer on *Yoga*, the sage Patanjali (about 150 B.C.), stated: "Yoga is the stopping of the spontaneous activities of the mind."

Yoga offers many methods of breath control. Each kind of breath control serves a certain purpose, just as yogic postures do.

YOGI

A *Yogi* is a person who subscribes to the yoga philosophy or doctrine. It is popularly assumed that a yogi has occult powers.

Z

Zen Buddhism
Zodiac
Zoroastrianism

ZEN BUDDHISM

Zen Buddhism first became a separate movement (*see* BUD-DHISM) in Japan in 1191 when a monk named Eisai founded the Rinzai school of Zen. Rinzai makes extensive use of the koans, or riddles, intended to "make the calculating mind die." A famous koan is: "What is the sound made by one hand clapping?"

Another example is the story of the monk who asked his master, "Who is the Buddha?" The answer was: "Three measures of flax."

The more popular form of Zen in Japan, the Soto school founded by Dogen, does not use koans. It employs meditation in a cross-legged position to attain *satori*, or enlightenment. Zen believes in achieving enlightenment through one's own efforts. It takes years of training in a monastery to become a Zen master. Zen is popular with laymen, who spend periods of retreat in Zen monasteries. The samurai (warrior class) valued its training in calming the mind amongst the dangers of the soldier's life.

Zen influenced landscape gardening, and the tea ceremony originated as a ritual of rest and refreshment after the strain of Zen meditation.

Both the Rinzai and Soto school of Zen believe in mind-to-mind instruction from master to disciple with the aim of awakening the Buddha-mind within everyone.

Comment: I remember my son coming into the kitchen one day with a smile on his face. He was in high school at the time. Someone had introduced Andrew to the concept of a koan. His hands are extremely flexible. He is able to flap one hand back and forth quickly enough so that his fingers smack audibly against the palm of his hand.

"Look Mom," he beamed, "the sound of one hand clapping."

We both had a good laugh.

ZODIAC

The *zodiac* is an imaginary belt in the celestial sphere, extending about eight degrees on either side of the ecliptic, the apparent annual path of the sun among the stars. The width of the zodiac was determined originally so as to include the orbits of the sun and moon, and of the five planets (Mercury, Venus, Mars, Jupiter, and Saturn) that were known at the time.

The zodiac is divided into twelve, thirty-degree sections which are called the signs of the zodiac. Starting with the vernal equinox, and proceeding eastward along the ecliptic, each of the divisions is named for the constellation situated within its limits in the second century B.C.

The names of the zodiacal signs are: Aries, the Ram; Taurus, the Bull; Gemini, the Twins; Cancer, the Crab; Leo, the Lion; Virgo, the Virgin; Libra, the Balance; Scorpio, the Scorpion; Sagittarius, the Archer; Capricornus, the Goat; Aquarius, the Water Bearer; and Pisces, the Fishes.

The zodiacal signs are believed by many authorities to have originated in Mesopotamia as early as 2000 B.C. According to that theory, the Greeks adopted the symbols from the Babylonians, and thereafter, the zodiac was passed on to the other ancient civilizations. The Egyptians assigned other names and symbols to the zodiacal divisions.

The Chinese also adopted the twelve-fold division, but called the signs respectively: rat, ox, tiger, hare, dragon, serpent, horse, sheep, monkey, hen, dog, and pig.

The Aztec Indians devised a similar system—apparently developed independently. (*Also see* HOROSCOPE.)

ZOROASTRIANISM

Zoroastrianism is the religious system founded by Zoroaster, who dates back to a time before Christ. He was the first to define and quantify spirits. He divided the spirit world into two forces—good and bad.

He also divided time into two categories: eternal time, and a span of 12,000 years within eternal time. The 12,000 years were divided into four sections of 3,000 years each. These quarters, in turn, had their own divisions; and the whole, formed a sort of cosmic clock, the smallest portion being twelve hours.

Zoroaster was the legislator and prophet of ancient Persia, and Zoroastrianism was the religion of the Persians previous to their conversion to Mohammedanism.

Bibliography

Alper, Dr. Frank, *Exploring Atlantis Volumes I, II, & III*. Thousand Oaks, California: Quantum Productions, 1981.

Begley, Sharon & Hager, Mary, "A Fantastic Voyage to Neptune," *Newsweek Magazine*. New York: Newsweek, Sept. 4, 1989.

Brennan, Barbara, *Hands of Light: A Guide to Healing Through the Human Energy Field*. New York: Bantam New Age, 1987.

Calhoun, Marcy, *Are You Really Too Sensitive?* Nevada City, CA: Blue Dolphin, 1987

Carpenter, Bruce & Krippner, Stanley Ph. D., "Spice Island Shaman: A Torajan Healer in Sulawesi," *Shaman's Drum: A Journal of Experiental Shamanism*. Number 18 Mid Fall. Berkeley, CA: Cross-Cultural Shamanism Network, 1989.

Cavendish, Richard, *The Great Religions*. London: Contact, 1980.

Cooke, Grace, *Meditation*. London: White Eagle Pub. Trust, 1955.

Dowling, Levi, *The Aquarian Gospel of Jesus the Christ*. Marina Del Rey, CA: De Vorss, 1987.

Garrett, Eileen J., *Awareness*. New York: Berkley Publishing, 1968.

Goodspeed, E.J., *The Apocrypha*. New York: Random House, 1959.

Humphreys, Christmas, *Zen: A Way of Life*. London: English Univ. Press, 1962.

Humphreys, Christmas. *Exploring Buddhism*. London: Allen & Unwin, 1974.

Jones, Alexander (General Editor), *The Jerusalem Bible Reader's Edition*. Garden City, NY: Doubleday, 1966.

Karlins, Marvin & Andrews, Lewis M., *Biofeedback*. New York: Warner, 1973.

Kuhlman, Kathryn, *I Believe In Miracles*. New York: Pyramid, 1962.

Lewis, Spencer H., *Rosicrucian Manual*. Kingsport, TN: Kingsport Press, 1966.

Maclaine, Shirley, *Going Within*. New York: Bantam Books, 1989.

MacDougall, Mary Katherine, *Happiness Now*. Unity Village, MI: Unity Books, 1971.

McGarey, William A. M.D., *The Edgar Cayce Remedies*. New York: Bantam Books, 1983.

Monroe, Robert, *Journeys Out of the Body*. Garden City, NY: Doubleday, 1971.

Montgomery, Ruth, with Garland, Joanne, *Ruth Montgomery: Herald of the New Age*. New York: Fawcett Crest, 1986.

Morvay, Alan, "A Shaman's Journey with Brant Secunda," *Shaman's Drum: A Journal of Experiental Shamanism*. Number 18 Mid Fall. Berkeley, CA: Cross-Cultural Shamanism Network, 1989.

Ostrander, Sheila & Schroeder, Lynn, *Psychic Discoveries Behind the Iron Curtain*. New York: Bantam Books, 1971.

Park, Willard Z., "The Acquisition of Power in Paviotso Shamanism," *Shaman's Drum: A Journal of Experiental Shamanism*. Number 18 Mid Fall. Berkeley, CA: Cross-Cultural Shamanism Network, 1989.

Parry, Danaan, *The Essene Book of Days*. Cooperstown, NY: Sunstone Publications, 1989.

Peschel, Lisa, *The Runes: Their Uses In Divination and Magick*. St. Paul, MN: Llewellyn Publications, 1989.

Roberts, Ursula, *Hints On Mediumistic Development*. London.

Rugush, Nicholas M., *The Human Aura*. New York: Berkley, 1974.

Silbey, Uma, *The Complete Crystal Guidebook*. Toronto: Bantam Books, 1987.

Spraggett, Allen, *Kathryn Kuhlman: The Woman Who Believes In Miracles*. Scarborough, Ontario: A Signet Book, 1970.

Van Gelder, Dora, *The Real World of Fairies*. Wheaton, IL: Quest, The Theosophical Publishing House, 1977.

Von Däniken, Erich, *Chariots of the Gods?* NY: Bantam Books, 1971.

Weaver Graham, *A to Z of the Occult*. London: Everest Books Limited, 1975.

Zolar, *Zolar's Encyclopedia and Dictionary of Dreams*. Garden City, NY: Doubleday, 1963.

Elaine Murray is the mother of two grown children: Andrew Murray, a lawyer and Heather Chwastiak, a teacher. An elementary school teacher, Elaine taught the primary grades for five years, took time out to raise her family, returned to teach a vocal music program for thirteen years, was widowed, and finally obtained her B.A. from the University of Western Ontario in 1985.

Her greatest passion is music and, when at home in Ontario, Elaine sings with a group of women called "The Treble Clefs." Were she more of a risk-taker, she would have tried "acting" as a career, but has enjoyed many roles on stage of the Simcoe Little Theatre. Mostly she misses feeding the mule deer from her days in British Columbia where she fed six to seven on a regular basis. "Two of them I coaxed to eat from my hand. There is nothing quite like the thrill of earning a wild animal's trust."

Now, together with her companion, Wesley Bethune, Elaine lives in southern Ontario in a little village called Turkey Point, and owns a vacation home on the ocean in Cape Breton Island, where she does most of her writing. She loves seagulls and feels most at home near the water. "My home in Turkey Point, Ontario faces Lake Erie where I watch the sun come up. My vacation home on Cape Breton faces the Gulf of St. Lawrence where I watch the sun set over the ocean."